4.26.78

STATE
GOVERNMENT

STATE
GOVERNMENT

JUDITH BENTLEY

American Government Series

Consulting Editor, Richard Darilek

Department of History
Herbert H. Lehman College
The City University of New York

Franklin Watts
New York | London | 1978

Cartoons courtesy of:

ROTHCO: (Ivey—Sentinel Star) p. 7; (Ivey—Orlando Evening Star) p. 48; (Renault—Sacramento Bee) pp. 16, 34; (Rothco Cartoons) p. 22; (Pearson—Knickerbocker News) pp. 26, 28; (Peterson—Vancouver Sun) p. 52; (Hy Rosen—Albany Times-Union) p. 87; (Margulies—Rothco Cartoons) p. 106.

Sidney Harris: pp. 41, 72.

Library of Congress Cataloging in Publication Data

Bentley, Judith.
  State government.

  (The American Government series)
  Bibliography: p.
  Includes index.
  SUMMARY: An overview of the history, structure, and operations of state governments with a discussion of issues facing the states such as federalism and interstate cooperation.
  1. State governments—Juvenile literature.
[1. State governments] I. Title.
JK2408.B46   320.9'73   77–14490
ISBN 0–531–01343–X

CONTENTS

2012063

STATE
GOVERNMENT

CHAPTER ONE

State Government: An Overview

The first important government in the United States was state government. After the skirmishes at Lexington and Concord, Massachusetts asked its fellow colonies to help fight the British, and the thirteen agreed to unite temporarily. But none were yet ready to give up the independence from each other they had enjoyed for one hundred fifty years. Not everyone agreed with Patrick Henry, who said at the First Continental Congress that he was no longer a Virginian but an American—that "the distinctions between Virginians, Pennsylvanians, New Yorkers, and New Englanders are no more."

Most of the colonies that made up the original thirteen had begun with a group of settlers or investors who received a grant of land from the king of England. Along with the grant came a charter extending the king's control to the new colony and a governor appointed by the king whose job was to enforce British law. In 1618 the governor of the Virginia colony decided to set up a local representative assembly. This group was the start of the future state legislatures, and of the governor's troubles.

Gradually the other colonies also developed assemblies and by 1763 the assemblies had gained some power. They had the right to tax the colonists, to select some officials such as the treasurer, to control schools and churches, and to raise troops and spend money on Britain's wars, if they chose to do so. The assemblies had begun to think of themselves as representing the colonists, rather than the British king.

During the Revolution the people's assemblies took control, threw out the royal governors, and elected representatives to the new Continental Congress. The representatives of the thirteen colonies agreed to unite in the effort to become "free and independent states," as they proclaimed in the Declaration of Independence. While the Congress was writing the Articles of Confederation, it urged the individual states to write their own new constitutions. Eleven of the thirteen did, and the governments set up by these constitutions became the models for later state governments.

THE STATE CONSTITUTIONS

In general, these new constitutions reflected the colonists' dislike of the royal governors by taking power from the governor and giving it to the assembly, or legislature. In fact, in most states the governor was selected by the legislature and was allowed to serve for only one year.

Most of the state legislatures had two houses, representing different segments of the population. To be elected to the upper house, a man had to be worth about $4,000. The lower house represented "the multitude," although there were sometimes property requirements for serving in it, too. Only the lower house could originate money bills. All legislators were elected for one-

or two-year terms. This short term was intended to make the assemblies more responsive to public opinion.

The state constitutions also made the legislature responsible for setting up the court system, and in most states the assemblies selected the judges themselves. Eight constitutions had bills of rights, but on the whole the state governments were not especially democratic. Pennsylvania's was the most radical; it did away altogether with the governor and the upper house. The group who wrote the constitution was described by one Pennsylvanian of the day as "a set of workmen," which was meant as an insult. This antidemocratic attitude was fairly common at the time.

In seven states the right to vote, called the suffrage, was given to every male taxpayer. The remaining states required moderate property ownership. Neither blacks, women, nor native American Indians living in the states were allowed to vote.

During the Revolution the states had put aside their differences, but after the victory over the British at Yorktown they began to fight among themselves. Claims to lands in the West, payment of war debts, and charges on goods passing through states were some of the subjects under dispute. George Washington wrote to James Madison in 1786, "We are fast verging to anarchy and confusion!" It was obvious the states would have to give up some of their independent ways for the common good.

THE FEDERAL CONSTITUTION

When the delegates from the states gathered in Philadelphia in 1787 to write a federal constitution, one of their major concerns was to decide how much power the individual states would have to give up, a problem that was difficult to settle. Eventually, the delegates did work out a compromise. The powers of government were divided between the national and state governments. This division of powers is called *federalism*. The national and state governments each have different powers and each level works for the most part independently.

POWERS GIVEN TO THE FEDERAL GOVERNMENT

- to conduct foreign relations
- to provide for national defense
- to issue currency
- to collect taxes on goods from other countries
- to regulate trade among the states

POWERS KEPT BY THE STATES

- to ratify constitutional amendments
- to determine voting requirements
- to hold elections
- to keep all the powers not specifically given to the national government or forbidden to the states. The most important was the "police" power, that is, the power to provide for (or "police") the health, welfare, safety, morals, and convenience of the people.

The Constitution and laws of the United States "shall be the Supreme Law of the land. . . ." This statement made it clear that in a conflict between national and state law, the national law would prevail. State officials would have to enforce acts of Congress. Further, the federal courts could find state laws *unconstitutional*; that is, they could declare that a state law was invalid because it conflicted with what was in the federal Constitution.

But the division of power between the two governments, state and national, was not completely spelled out in the Constitution. From time to time the Supreme Court has to make decisions that clarify what power belongs to what level of government. In general, the idea has been followed that the states gave to the national government only those powers that it really needed. They kept all the rest, including those that most closely affected the people. James Madison said the states would control "all the objects which in the ordinary course of affairs, concern the lives, liberties, and properties of the people. . . ."

STATE RESPONSIBILITIES TODAY

The states today have a great influence on the ordinary lives of their citizens. It is the state government that a person most often deals with in the affairs of everyday life. In general, state government is responsible for:

- building hospitals, public housing, highways, state universities, parks, and recreation areas
- administering unemployment payments and some part of health care and welfare payments
- setting standards for teachers, doctors, dentists, nurses, food handling, automobile driving, milk production, insurance, banking, public utilities (such as electricity), and air and water purity
- running state universities, mental hospitals, state courts, prisons and rehabilitation centers, and employment services

In addition, the states control the system of justice and law enforcement most people come in contact with. Murder, robbery, automobile accidents, marijuana use, child adoption, changing one's name, marriage, divorce—all of these are concerns of state government.

The states need money to carry on all these activities. As state responsibilities have grown, state taxes have grown too. Up until the late 1930s most states relied on the tax on property (land, houses, other buildings) as their principal source of income. When this proved inadequate, many states added sales and income taxes. By 1973 all but five states had an income tax on individuals, all but four an income tax on businesses. But the sales tax—including taxes on gasoline, tobacco, and alcoholic beverages—accounts for more than half of all state revenues.

By increasing spending and raising taxes, the states have managed to remain largely responsible for the lives of their citizens, though there have been shifts of power in federal-state relations. The states were dominant for the first one hundred years, then the federal government expanded its power for the next seventy years. Some people feel that during the last thirty years the states have been regaining power.

This federal-state relationship—a unique quality of American government—has always had a great impact on state government. To a large extent it controls what state government is like and what it can do. Let's take a closer look at the history of this relationship.

FEDERAL-STATE RELATIONS

During the first hundred years of United States history the states did most of the governing that directly affected the people. The national government concentrated on foreign affairs. In a pattern called "dual federalism," each level of government controlled its own sphere as set out in the Constitution. But during this relatively quiet period, some problems were developing. The problems erupted into the Civil War, a dispute over who had "sovereignty," the national or state government.

The word *sovereignty* means having supreme political power and authority. The Civil War once and for all settled the question in favor of the national government. A series of constitutional amendments passed after the war clarified this, spelling out the

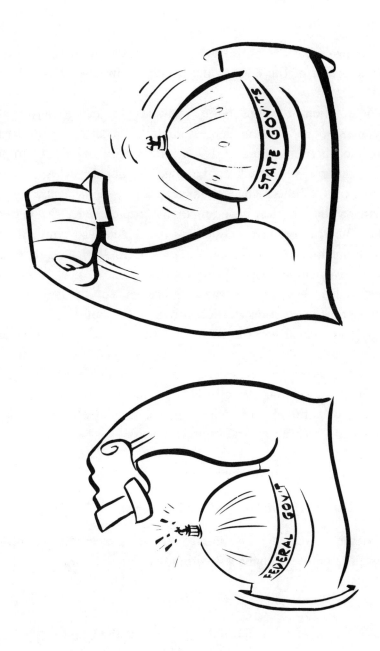

federal government's control over social and economic policy and the protection of the civil rights of citizens in case of attack by the states.

The question of "states' rights," however, has never really died. In contemporary political debates there often arises a difference of opinion between those of a "liberal" political stand and those of a "conservative" stand. In general, the liberal favors government action to effect changes in people's lives; the conservative maintains that the less government in people's lives, the better. When liberals propose action by the federal government in some problem area, usually by citing the Civil War amendments, conservatives often respond that such action is a violation of states' rights. The antisegregation movement of the late 1950s, particularly the voter-registration drives in the South, provide an example of federal government action that stirred a cry of violation of states' rights from conservative opponents. In addition to civil rights, urban problems and environmental issues often provoke disputes in which states' rights are invoked. These issues, of course, are continually affected by judicial decisions that interpret the federal Constitution and its amendments.

THE CIVIL WAR AMENDMENTS

The Thirteenth Amendment (1865)

"Neither slavery nor involuntary servitude, except as a punishment for crime . . . shall exist within the United States."

The Fourteenth Amendment (1868)

"All persons born or naturalized in the United States . . . are citizens of the United States. . . . No State shall make or enforce any law which shall abridge the privileges or immunities of citizens of the United States; nor shall any State deprive any person of life, liberty, or property, without due process of law; nor deny to any person within its jurisdiction the equal protection of the laws."

The Fifteenth Amendment (1870)

"The right of citizens of the United States to vote shall not be denied or abridged by the United States or by any State on account of race, color, or previous condition of servitude."

From 1860 on, dual federalism continued, but the pendulum of power was swinging back to the federal government's side. The state government's power to regulate business—including working conditions in factories, the health and safety of workers, and wages and hours—was held back. The Supreme Court interpreted the word "person" in the Fourteenth Amendment to mean corporations, and protected the corporations from state regulation. Thus, state governments, which were unable to combat corruption, came under the control of political machines and big business. Between 1866 and 1872, for example, the Union Pacific Railroad spent $400,000 on political bribes in the states and the office of United States senator was auctioned by the legislatures to the highest bidder.

At the turn of the century the states attempted to regain their leadership. Hiram Johnson, California governor at the time, said the states should "kick the corporations out of politics." A "progressive" movement that aimed to do just this started in California under Johnson, in New Jersey under Governor Woodrow Wilson, in New York with Theodore Roosevelt, and in Wisconsin with Robert La Follette. States passed progressive laws protecting workers and establishing transportation, industrial, and public utilities commissions to fix rates and supervise services. The states also began to initiate internal reforms and to spend more money for state activities.

The depression of the 1930s brought a halt to the renewed vitality of the states, who were totally unable to cope with the massive economic problems of the time. As President, Franklin D. Roosevelt introduced a "New Deal" to combat the depression. Dual federalism gave way to what he called "cooperative" federalism. Instead of assigning specific functions to each level of government, he would get all three of them—national, state, and local—moving on specific programs. In truth, most of the ideas and resources came from the national government, which began bypassing the states and providing relief directly to local governments. Seventy-five percent of the relief funds spent between 1933 and 1937 were spent by the national government.

Since World War II both the federal and state governments have rapidly expanded both their activities and their expenditures. Distinctions between the federal-state system have become fuzzier. Although they are not now dominating the national government, the states may be said to be regaining power by becoming much more active than before. State expenditures have multiplied since 1950 from $11 billion to $78 billion in 1973; along with local expenditures, they now account for more than 60 percent of all public domestic spending. During the same period, federal aid to state and local governments increased from $2.5 billion to $39 billion. Most of this spending goes for new highways, welfare payments, and education.

The Great Society programs under President Lyndon Johnson in the 1960s promoted a more direct sharing of federal money and responsibility with local community groups, leaving out the states once again. The national government began to be involved in new areas such as air and water pollution, mass transportation, and development of the cities.

In the 1970s President Richard Nixon introduced revenue-sharing—the direct return of federal income taxes to state and local governments. Over the five-year period from 1972 to 1977,

$30.2 billion was returned to the states to be used for any legal expenditures. Revenue-sharing grew out of a renewed feeling that the governments closest to the people could do the best job of governing and out of a desire to cut down on the size and activity of the federal government.

THE QUALITY OF STATE GOVERNMENT

How good state governments have been in responding to the needs of their citizens has varied a great deal in different times and places. The internal strength of a state government is largely determined by its state constitution. Unfortunately, state constitutions have not kept up with changing demands.

As new states enter the Union, they are required only to have a republican (a representative) form of government. Most of the states entering before the Civil War copied the constitutions of the original states. As we have seen, these governments featured a strong legislature and a relatively weak governor. Around 1830, the state governments were made more democratic as voting rights were extended to more people. An increasing number of state officials, including judges, were put on a ballot that got longer and longer. The idea behind the so-called long ballot was that having officeholders elected rather than appointed by the governor made them more responsible to the people.

In the post–Civil War period—when twenty-four of the present state constitutions were written—a reaction against strong legislatures had set in. This reaction was caused in large part by the corruption in the legislatures and their domination by big business.

The constitutions written at this time took as much government activity as possible "out of politics." Legislative sessions were scheduled for every two years instead of yearly. The number of days each session might meet was limited. The less time spent at the state house, the less damage could be done, voters seemed to feel.

These constitutions also set financial limits on such things as the state debt, tax rates, and salaries of state officials. Voting rights were restricted again. Connecticut and Massachusetts, for example, added literacy tests for voters.

While the legislature was weakened, the governorship was strengthened. The office was made directly elective by the people and the term extended from one year to two or four years. At the beginning of the twentieth century, reforms in the general functioning of state governments were also proposed. Such procedures as requiring primary elections to select candidates for office, placing large public issues on the ballot for a public vote, and using merit qualifications to select state employees have been gradually adopted by the states. These measures give the people more control and improve the quality of their government.

Still there has not been full-scale change in the structure and working of state governments. Change has come about slowly. The states have been forced to earn back gradually the respect and strength they had in colonial times.

We have seen the foundation of state governments, laid before the birth of the United States itself. We have traced the activities of these governments to modern times and the changes written into their constitutions in different periods, and we have seen the swing of influence back and forth between the states and the federal government. In the next few chapters we will examine in more detail the actual functioning of these state governments.

CHAPTER TWO

The Executive Branch

When state governments were founded, the citizens didn't want a powerful executive. But today, the office of the governor—the state's highest executive position—has become the predominant force in state government. As the legislatures grew less powerful in the nineteenth century, the office of governor took over as the prime mover of state policy. In doing this, the governorship passed through several stages: from a powerless executive during the nation's first seventy years, to the businessman's or political-party dominated governor of the last half of the nineteenth century, and finally to the modern governor. Today's governors often show independence from political-party organization by appealing directly to the people for support. They more efficiently control the administration of state government, and many governors now spend a large portion of their time on national affairs. They testify before Congressional committees, work with other governors, and are influential in national politics.

"I WILL EXPLAIN OUR DECISION-MAKING PROCESS ---"

However, governors have not become as strong in their states as the President is in the nation. Their influence is restricted by constitutional limits, personality factors, political forces, and their relationship with their legislatures. The organization of the state government and the quality of state workers also affect the governor's strength.

THE POWERS OF THE GOVERNOR

Constitutionally, governors found a new source of strength when direct popular election replaced election by the legislature. Direct election by the people gives the governor a statewide base of support. Also, the governor's term has gradually been lengthened from one year, as provided in the first state constitutions, to four years. (Exceptions are Arkansas, New Hampshire, Rhode Island, and Vermont.) Eight states forbid reelection, however, and nineteen limit the governor to two successive terms. In practice, this means that the governor has a relatively short time to put an imprint on state policy.

Powers now given to governors include, except in North Carolina, the right to veto legislation passed by the legislature (a two-thirds majority of the elected members may vote to override the veto); the right to address the legislature and recommend legislation; and the right to call special sessions of the legislature.

One provision that weakens the chief executive is the long ballot, as discussed in the first chapter. Executive departments that have elected administrators limit governors' control; these departments become semi-independent. In a 1966 survey governors said they felt particularly weak in appointive powers and in the right to reorganize the executive branch.

In addition to constitutional factors, the personality of the governor makes a difference in his or her performance. An effective governor must be a good politician—assertive, independent, and able to influence or even manipulate other people. Cracking heads together and making trouble for someone who interferes with set policies are part of a governor's techniques. The most effective leaders, said one political scientist in a discussion about New Jersey governors, "have been men of driving ambition and fierce concentration, who pursue their goals relentlessly."

"From the first day of a legislative session until adjournment," commented former New Jersey governor Walter E. Edge, "I applied constant pressure in every legitimate manner to get the administration bills passed."

Political realities also affect the governorship. Governors usually become the leaders of their state party, although most governors are not in office long enough to develop their own political organizations. When elected they may name a new state chairperson for the party and then work closely with this person gathering legislative and electoral support. And because the governor's activities are reported in the press, he or she can use this exposure to gain more support for policies. Every appearance at a local barbecue or bridge dedication is an opportunity to promote the party's program and candidates.

Governors use "patronage" to build their political positions. In most states the executive has the power to appoint about half of the major administrative positions, subject to some degree of approval by the legislature. And although 54 percent of state employees are under the civil service system, the governor usually has several hundred lesser positions to fill, too. Patronage is most effectively used in the first year of the governor's term; as jobs are filled the governor has less to offer.

In addition to jobs, the governor can also hand out "pork": construction contracts for roads, parks, and hospitals, state insurance contracts, and so on.

Modern governors rely less on patronage than their predecessors did. They do not want to offend the opposition party beyond repair, as they may need its support on a crucial vote one day.

The governors' constitutional powers, personality, and political clout all influence their relationship with the legislature. This relationship is crucial to the success of their programs. In the 1966 survey mentioned before, governors indicated that working with the legislative branch was a considerable problem for them.

By far the greatest clout the governor has with the legislature is control of the budget. Most states use the executive budget. The governor and staff prepare a statement of projected income and spending that reflects the importance the administration gives to different activities. The legislature in its turn approves or disapproves parts of the budget.

A governor's budget-making powers vary from state to state. In Connecticut, for example, Governor Ella T. Grasso was able to choose her own commissioner of finance from out of state, who then became her budget-axer. The commissioner drew up a $1.68 billion budget that reflected Governor Grasso's priorities—a tough line on spending increases and a $125 million increase in taxes. Despite the pressures of liberal and labor groups, Grasso refused to propose a state income tax and instead raised and extended the sales tax to 7 percent, increased the tax on corporate income, and taxed stock dividends. Because her party—the Democrats—dominated the legislature, her budget passed relatively easily.

THE GOVERNOR'S PROGRAM

When the governor tries to promote the program on which he or she campaigned, the strengths or weaknesses of the office, and those of the person, come into play. Let us say, for instance, that a governor had promised to start a new system of community colleges in the state, and had promised to do it without raising taxes. Soon after the election the governor will confer with the commissioner of education. Even if the commissioner is not this governor's appointee, he or she is likely to favor the program since it means an expansion of the education department. The commissioner may offer practical advice as to what should be included in the legislation setting up the new colleges.

At the same time, the governor will try to build support among professional educators and the students who will attend the colleges. The governor probably wooed these voters in the campaign with a promise of the college system. The governor will also talk to county chairpeople of his or her party, telling them that one of the colleges might be built in their county if there is enough political support in the legislature for the project.

As the governor's staff drafts the legislation for the college system, the governor looks at the budget to find ways to finance it. Budget experts may suggest a bond issue to finance construction costs. (By issuing bonds, a government borrows money that must be paid back with interest to the individual or organization that loaned the money.) The cost of operating the colleges might be paid out of a tax on liquor sales, for instance. Some states are now using lotteries to raise money for education costs.

The governor addresses both houses of the legislature shortly after inauguration and presents a program. The community college system is one of the new proposals. The project comes as no surprise to the leaders of the legislature, and they direct the proposed legislation to the appropriate committee. Few legislators of either party really oppose this college project, but several members of the opposition party speak out against it. They say they are representing the views of educators concerned that the colleges will take funds from younger students' programs. The governor may be forced to compromise by cutting down on the size of the project or by finding new funds for it.

Meanwhile, the governor holds press conferences attacking the legislative opposition, makes appearances all over the state to publicize the bill, and offers a few patronage plums to reluctant legislators in return for their votes. With persistence, luck, and strong public support, the governor will get the community colleges he or she wants—and the political credit for establishing them.

The responsibility for putting into effect programs and budgets approved by the legislature lies with the governor, for in addition to being the chief legislators of their states, governors are also the chief administrators. Few can afford to spend much time in this role. It has been estimated that only 10 percent of a governor's time is spent talking with department heads (as compared to about 20 percent one governor said he spent testifying before Congressional committees). Instead, governors rely on their staffs to handle the daily activities and to bring to their attention only major problems.

REORGANIZATION PLANS

Many of the attempts to strengthen state government have concentrated on reorganizing the executive branch to make it more efficient and more responsive to the governor. Because many executive agencies were formed in the late nineteenth century during the movement to take government "out of politics," there are now a variety of executive departments headed by a variety of administrators. The position of superintendent of instruction or commissioner of education was made an elected position in many states, for example, so that education would be more directly in the hands of the people. As a result, education departments, which now spend more than one-third of general state and local revenues and employ 40 percent of all state employees, are usually the most independent departments.

Highway departments, which are often second in expenditures

"We envision a six-lane expressway which will enable four times as many cars to enjoy this unspoiled scenic drive twice as fast . . ."

and third in number of employees (hospitals are second), usually have an appointed head. The highway department is a rich source of patronage and contracts for the governor to give out. Newer agencies, such as labor, banking, and health, are more likely to have an administrator appointed by the governor. As a result, they tend to be less independent. Some executive boards and agencies choose their own heads; still others are appointed by the legislature. And in addition to the major departments, states may have temporary commissions to investigate and make recommendations on problems, and authorities with limited functions such as maintaining a bridge or tunnel.

The number of agencies makes them unmanageable; every time there is a new problem—pollution, urban decay, faltering mass transportation—there is a tendency to create a new agency. Former governor Mark Hatfield described the situation in his state: "Oregon has an archaic organization which makes administration exceedingly difficult. We have in excess of 100 different boards, agencies, and commissions that report to the governor."

One way to make the executive branch more controllable is to put the agencies together into a few major departments—such as health, welfare, education, prisons, transportation, and recreation—under single appointed administrators, but attempts to do this often meet considerable resistance from the clientele or profession the agency serves. Agriculture and education are often most successful at maintaining their independence from the governor because of the strong support they receive from farmers and teachers.

EXECUTIVE APPOINTMENTS

Another way to increase the governor's control besides reorganization is to abolish the long ballot. The governor then appoints a larger number of state officials. Positions that are usually elective in most states include lieutenant governor, secretary of state, attorney general, treasurer, and auditor. But some states elect many more. Michigan elects thirty-six different officials.

The disadvantage of the long ballot is that the governor may have been elected by a broad majority of the people but if the other officials running on the same ticket are defeated, the governor may not have working control of the government. Only eighteen states even specify that the governor and lieutenant governor run as a team. Each elected official is constitutionally independent of the governor and under no legal obligation to cooperate.

Although few positions have been added to the ballot recently, it is difficult to remove a position from it. There is still good reason, of course, for electing some officials directly, especially those who oversee the finances. The auditor, for example, has the power to determine whether a department's spending is in line with what the legislature decides.

REGULATORY AGENCIES

There is a good argument for electing members of the agencies that perform regulatory functions. Such boards or commissions act almost as judges to regulate business, labor, public utilities, and license the professions. If these agencies are to be objective and impartial, they must be as independent as possible. Usually, elected officials are the most independent.

Regulating is often performed poorly. Public service commissions have difficulty determining what a reasonable and fair profit is. Conflict of interest occurs when board members own utilities stock. Boards regulating the professions become so closely allied with their clientele that the board neglects the public interest and instead promotes the welfare of the profession. States are often

ACTIVITIES REGULATED BY THE STATES

Business	Labor	Utilities	Professions
Manufacture of drugs	Regulation of hours	Distribution of electricity and gas	Establishing standards for medical and teaching professions
Preparation of food	Minimum wage	Public transportation	
Issuing insurance	Child labor		
Establishing banks and business corporations	Right to strike	Public communication	Accrediting schools, colleges, and professional schools
	Unemployment compensation		
Pollution control	Injury and disability compensation		
Protection from fraud (the blue-sky laws to prevent selling shares in the "bright blue sky itself")	Discrimination in employment		Licensing insurance agents
Sale of liquor			
Gambling and racing			

reluctant to force companies to control pollution, regulate factory conditions, or provide adequate unemployment insurance. They do not want to drive companies to move to states with less rigid controls. Several insurance companies have central offices in Hartford, Connecticut, for example, a state where controls on the insurance business are weak.

On the other hand, states can be more effective regulators than the federal government. California's Air Resources Board fined American Motors Corporation $4.2 million in 1976 for not meeting the state's strict automobile-pollution-control standards.

Do any of the new consumer protection agencies protect us from the government?

STATE EMPLOYEES

The performance of the executive branch is largely determined by the people who work for it. Because salaries are generally lower than those offered by the private sector and because so many of the chores are unglamorous, state government often fails to attract the best people in a field. Most jobs, from a public works wage-investigator to an engineering geologist, have been covered by civil service since the 1930s. Civil service has been criticized for promoting mediocrity and for excluding top professionals, who are seldom willing to take an exam or go through the bureaucratic maze in order to be hired. But federal health and welfare programs administered by the states contain the provision that personnel be chosen on the merit principle. And under the 1940 Hatch Act employees must remain politically neutral while holding a government position.

In the meantime, patronage has become less prevalent for some of the same reasons—low salaries and unattractive jobs. Huge turnovers in the bureaucracies with a change in party control of the statehouse are less common now than in the past.

At the very top level of state government there have been signs of vitality as fresh blood is attracted—often temporarily—to areas such as environmental protection, urban planning, and mass transit. Once an administrator has been in office for a while he or she develops an expertise that is superior to that of elected officials. Departments can become important sources of new ideas and information, definers of social needs, and proposers of solutions to the legislature or governor.

In summary, the executive branch, in performing a wide variety of services, is loosely coordinated by the governor, though some departments maintain a strong sense of independence or are responsive to other interests. The modern governor has assumed a

He wants to know why we
don't hire on merit.
What's merit?

greater role in policy leadership and in running the overall business of the state. His or her effectiveness may be limited, however, by constitutional restrictions, personality, political forces, the relationship with the legislature, the organization of the administration, and the quality of state personnel.

CHAPTER THREE

The Legislature

State legislatures have fallen low since their heyday as the "popular branch" of government early in United States history. In fact, they have been blamed for a large share of the falling prestige of the states. "By . . . not legislating on vital public interest issues," says former Iowa governor Harold E. Hughes, "a state legislature can effectively preserve the status quo and keep a state in the ox-cart era."

In theory, the legislature has four basic functions: to pass laws, to control expenditures, to oversee the executive, and to represent the citizenry in the most direct manner. But in practice, these functions have dwindled until the legislature merely approves or disapproves the governor's legislative program rather than initiating its own. It goes along with the budget drafted by the executive branch rather than drafting its own, approves executive actions routinely, and often represents the interests of some parts of the community at the expense of others.

"BY THE PUREST COINCIDENCE, LADIES AND GENTLEMEN,
I WAS JUST ABOUT TO WRITE A PROPERTY TAX RELIEF BILL!"

THE QUALITY OF LEGISLATIVE PERFORMANCE

With respect to the lawmaking function, Governor Hughes says, "Our legislatures have traditionally governed not so much by legislating as by *not* legislating." Bills that are really bad usually don't get passed, but bills that are good and important don't pass either. Instead, the legislature deals in trivia, often spending more time debating the state insect (North Carolina rejected the bedbug) than deciding whether the sales tax should apply to medicine.

In deciding what legislation to consider, the legislature responds to external pressures from the governor, administrative agencies, interest groups, or local supporters. In theory, as part of its lawmaking function, the legislature should bring problems to public attention. It should educate the public on the issues involved. In practice, no more than 5 percent of the bills introduced arouse enough public attention to make the legislator's vote politically important. Many are rushed through without any debate at all in the last few, hectic days of the session. And most bills are passed without a single negative vote because they involve only local or minor matters. 2012063

Legislation has the best chance of passing when influential groups support it and the public becomes intensely concerned. It also does well if parties and powerful legislators support the legislation and if there is no strong and organized opposition.

The legislature is responsible for controlling the money spent, but the executive budget system limits the effectiveness of the lawmakers. The governor has most of the initiative and most of the power. Legislatures seldom propose new spending for pioneering programs. Their action on the budget is more likely to be to cut here and there and concentrate on "holding the line" on spending. They are generally poorly staffed and thus cannot properly analyze the budget presented to them.

To oversee the executive branch, the legislature has several powers it can use: giving out or withholding of funds, approving or disapproving of appointments to high-level positions, and holding committee hearings or investigations. However, in practice, few funds are ever withheld, few appointments are ever rejected, and little successful legislation has resulted from committee hearings or investigations.

Lawmakers feel they are best at performing the fourth function, that of representing the citizenry. The people who live in the district represented by a legislator are called constituents. To help constituents, legislators may sponsor "local bills" relating to their country or district, run various errands among government offices, intercede before administrative agencies, and provide entertainment when voters visit the state capital.

Constituent service comes naturally to the legislators because of the deep roots they have in the communities they represent, such as membership in community organizations, lifetime residencies, and shared religious and ethnic affiliations. They are the most truly representative officials in the state government since their concern is only to represent a small, relatively homogeneous segment of the state. It is said that legislators "vote their constituencies." This can be both a strength and a handicap.

In addition to doing their legislative job insufficiently, legislatures suffer from a bad press. Ever since the Yazoo Land Fraud of 1795—when the Georgia legislature was bribed by a group of speculators to sell fifty million acres of state land at a penny an acre—the taint of corruption has been hard to shake. Too many opportunities present themselves.

Although outright bribery has become rare, less obvious forms of corruption survive. Illinois state senator Paul Simon estimated that one-third of the legislators in his state take payoffs, either as payment for legal or public relations services or as campaign contributions.

Another reason for the legislatures' poor reputation is that for a long time representation of all citizens of the state was not equal. There was seldom any reapportioning of seats in the legislature to match changes in the size of the population in a geographic area. Before the reapportionment movement of the 1960s, rural areas that had lost people to the cities still held the same number of legislators. The growing cities never gained any representatives. Thus, rural areas dominated the legislatures out of all proportion to their share of the population. In 1960 the number of people represented in house districts in Vermont varied from thirty-eight to thirty-five thousand. In California the number of people represented in senate districts ranged from fourteen thousand to six million.

This meant, for instance, that New York's upstate "appleknockers," as they were called, held back New York City politicians. Florida's pinewoods senators controlled the city slickers from Miami and Tampa. And downstaters in Illinois overruled Chicago. In many states with consistently Democratic governors, the Republicans kept control of one or both houses of the legislature. Alfred E. Smith, governor of New York in the 1920s, once complained that the legislature was "constitutionally Republican."

However, state legislatures are now showing unmistakable signs of life. As a result of reapportionment, urban areas have gained in influence. Los Angeles County, for instance, went from one to fourteen seats in the California senate. Republicans have become stronger in the South, producing something of a revival of the two-party system there. And the minorities, especially the blacks, have gained representatives, and some influential ones. In Connecticut a public interest group drew up profiles of all the legislators, making their views and actions better known to the public.

This quiet comeback is due, for the most part, to steady, gradual, internal reform during the past fifteen years. The legislature in many states has strived to assert itself as an equal and independent partner of the executive branch. California has developed the most professional and probably the best legislature in American history. What makes a legislature good? A closer look at how they operate should provide some of the answers.

THE LEGISLATURE AT WORK

All states except Nebraska have a bicameral, or two-house, legislature. The upper house was traditionally based on area and the lower house on population. But a 1964 Supreme Court decision said that both houses must be based on population. Legislatures vary in size from 49 members in Nebraska to 424 in New Hampshire. The larger-sized legislatures find it difficult to pay, equip, and staff themselves properly. In the newer state governments in the West, the lower house usually has fewer than 100 members, and this is generally regarded as a more workable size. Smaller size also makes the votes of individual legislators more important and better known to the public.

Forty-two legislatures now have regular annual sessions; the rest are held every two years. And legislatures now tend to remain in session longer than the sixty- and ninety-day limits imposed in the late nineteenth century. Those whose constitutions still specify a certain number of days use such devices as convening a special session or "covering the clock" so that time doesn't run out. California has a continuous two-year legislature; Michigan, New Jersey, and Pennsylvania also meet virtually year-round. On the other hand, Alabama's legislature meets for only thirty-six days every two years.

Legislative sessions are basically informal. A third of the states do not even provide printed copies of the bills on which legislators are expected to act. Although legal advice may be available from the attorney general's office for drafting bills, reference services or legal counsel are seldom provided to aid the legislator once a bill has been introduced. The operation of a session is usually sloppy at best and chaotic at worst. The last days, especially, begin to take on a circus atmosphere as bills are rushed through in an effort to beat the clock. Electronic improvements such as vote-recording machines and devices that track down relevant statutes automatically have improved the efficiency of proceedings, but simpler, clearer rules of procedures and a streamlining of sessions are still needed.

Most of a session's business is accomplished in committees. Every bill is assigned to a committee. The number and nature of the committees vary from state to state. They were once so specialized in Minnesota that the lower house had a committee on binding twine and one on railroad sleeping cars. In most legislatures the committee on committees, which makes assignments, and the rules committee, which decides when bills will be considered by the entire house, are the most important.

Once a bill has been introduced and referred to a committee, the committee decides whether to recommend it to the whole session. If it does, the bill is placed on the calendar by the rules committee, which is usually controlled by the majority party and can favor the bills it wants passed. The legislature usually adopts what the committees recommend, but the majority of bills never return to the general legislature. (The Florida senate once had a judiciary committee that was known as the Killer Committee.) Thus, most legislative decisions are made behind the scenes by a small number of legislators.

If the effectiveness of the legislature is to be improved, one place to begin is with these committees. In theory, they should have the expertise necessary to evaluate the governor's programs critically and start important legislation themselves. The major changes necessary are a reduction in the number of standing committees, a reduction in the number of assignments for legislators, larger and more competent staffs, more open, more democratic, and more efficient procedures with recorded and published roll-call votes, and adequate facilities for meetings and hearings. Committees would naturally become more effective if their members continued to serve on the same committees from one session to another and developed expertise.

THE PEOPLE WHO ARE THE LEGISLATORS

Leadership in the legislature usually falls to the political party in control, although party loyalties are less important and influential in the states than in the national Congress. The presiding officers may exert leadership. In the lower house the speaker is usually selected by a caucus, or meeting, of the majority party. The speaker, who also appoints the standing committees, is usually a strong leader.

In the upper house the lieutenant governor presides, but has less influence because he or she is not usually chosen by the legislature and also does not have appointive powers. The majority leader of the dominant party does wield power because he or she controls the appointments of committee chairpeople and the allotment of funds to committees.

How well a legislature performs is determined greatly by who the legislators are. The typical Democratic legislator comes from a low-income district in a city, the Republican from a rural or upper-income suburban or city district. More than half of all legislators are replaced every other year (although only a third of these have lost an election). This means that most legislators are amateurs, who follow the directions of the leaders. Terms of service are usually for four years in the upper houses. In the lower houses the terms are mostly for only two years. Longer terms in both houses would reduce the need for almost constant campaigning and make legislators more professional and experienced.

The nature of the legislature has a strong influence on the type of people who serve in it. Because the work is low-paying it has

"JUST BETWEEN US, FORBES — HOW <u>DOES</u> A BILL BECOME A LAW."

traditionally attracted the well-to-do, who could afford to serve and who have a sense of social obligation (or who see it as a way to protect their wealth), or farmers who have spare time after the fall harvest. More recently, lawyers and business people have begun to predominate.

Gradually, as the job becomes full-time and higher-paying, there may be a shift to the type of legislator who views legislative service as a career in itself. Longer terms that offer more job security would also make the job more attractive.

During 1972 and 1973 the average annual salary of legislators was $7,260. California and New York are on top, paying over $20,000 each. New Hampshire and Rhode Island are the lowest at $100 and $300 annually. Some states supplement salaries with expense allowances.

But there are ways to improve the legislatures other than making the job of legislator more attractive. The legislatures must begin policing themselves. Legislators are particularly open to conflicts of interest because they usually have another job. Many are lawyers and may be asked, for example, to represent a client before a state commission. The commission, of course, would be aware of the influence carried by the legislator-lawyer. Bankers are frequently found on the banking committees, and legislators who work for insurance companies may be helping to write the codes that regulate their own industry.

Legislatures have been encouraged to adopt codes of ethics that would include such points as full public disclosure of financial and business interests, optional self-disqualification in possible conflict-of-interest situations, and prohibition of lawyer-legislators from representing clients in hearings before administrative commissions.

In addition, legislatures must dust off and polish up some of their formal powers. In the area of policymaking they must seize some initiative from the executive and get out in front on some issues. The California legislature has taken the lead in this. Thirty-five years ago the governor of California had a "hot line" telephone installed at the assembly speaker's rostrum so that he could deliver his orders personally. One day the speaker ceremoniously yanked out the wires; the legislature has been asserting itself ever since. One thing it has done is to provide research staffs that come up with information independently so that the legislature can initiate policy and criticize the governor's program intelligently. The California assembly has its own Office of Research, whose sixteen professionals take a comprehensive look at state problems and make recommendations for action. The office provided the impetus for the Mental Health Act of 1967, the Pure Air Act of 1968, and legislation in the areas of smog prevention, unemployment, criminal deterrence, and gun control. The research office worked with the assembly's Transportation and Commerce Committee and came up with the strongest emission-control law in the nation after concluding that 90 percent of California smog was due to auto exhaust.

Aside from internal qualities, attention and public support affect how good a legislature is. If legislatures are to continue increasing their strength, they will need greater interest from the public. Public support will allow them to develop larger and more active staffs that will make legislators capable of more professional work in complicated matters.

One way of involving the public in lawmaking is through the "initiative," which twenty states have, and the "referendum," which twenty-two have. The initiative places a new proposal on the ballot. The referendum asks the voters to approve or disapprove a law that has already been passed by the legislature. A certain number of voters' signatures are required to put an initiative on the ballot. This makes initiatives expensive—$200,000 if you hire signature collectors in California. They are also vulnerable to exploitation by special interests who can afford to finance the petition-making process and the mass advertising campaign that usually follows.

In the area of financial responsibility the legislatures have attempted to increase their budgetary independence by creating their own budget staffs. All but four legislatures have some staff for analyzing the state budget; thirty-four have specialized agencies.

In the area of overseeing the executive branch, legislatures are taking more of the responsibility for checking up on finances of state agencies. Of sixty-one audit agencies in the fifty states (some states have two), thirty-six are selected by and report to the legislature. Legislatures have recently expanded this checking up to include an evaluation of the agencies' performances and the effectiveness of their programs.

Thus, the future for the legislature looks better and better. Whether the rest of the states will follow the practices begun by a few will determine just how strong the legislatures become.

CHAPTER FOUR

The Judiciary

The judicial branch of state government suddenly becomes important to the ordinary citizen when he or she has to go to court to fight a traffic ticket, get a divorce, probate a will, defend against an eviction, or identify a participant in a crime. The experience will probably not be a pleasant one. Defendants without lawyers mill around in crowded hallways trying to figure out the legal proceedings. A small noisy trial room is presided over by an unsympathetic clerk. A judge dulled by the repetition of routine cases nods behind the bench, and a less than deliberate, even-handed brand of justice is quickly dispensed. Although state courts vary from excellent to poor in quality, the vast majority are decidedly mediocre.

The state courts—more than the Supreme Court of the United States or the federal courts—determine the quality of justice meted out to the average person. State law is the basic law of the land. Federal courts deal primarily with matters of interstate

LAOCOON

commerce, protection of civil rights, assurance of due process, and federal crimes such as bank robbery and kidnapping across state lines. State-run courts handle everything else.

Most state criminal law follows the traditions of the British criminal code that was adopted by the American colonies. The twelve-person jury of one's peers, for example, is one of these. Criminal law in the United States has changed only slightly over two centuries. Usually only technical changes are made, such as in the classification of crimes (felonies are more serious crimes, misdemeanors are less serious crimes) or in the penalties to be imposed. More substantial changes—such as whether to eliminate capital punishment or to make marijuana use legal—may be debated in public for a long time before any agreement is reached to change the law.

A wide variety of types of cases are covered by state civil law: protection against fraud in business transactions, liability suits, building code violations, divorce, the probation of wills, traffic and parking violations, tenant evictions, adoption, negligence as in automobile accidents or medical malpractice, marriage, and mortgage defaults. The highest state courts also hear cases questioning the constitutionality of state laws.

In addition to the cases handled by the courts, state agencies handle civil complaints arising from the state's regulating functions. A state human rights commission, for example, may hear sex- or race-discrimination complaints; worker's compensation disputes may be heard by a state board; and pollution-control guidelines may be enforced by a state environmental protection agency.

STATE COURT SYSTEMS

Each state sets up its own court system, and there are a staggering number and variety of courts. Municipal courts, county courts, superior, circuit, and district courts, appellate courts, appellate divisions, courts of appeal, and supreme courts are all to be found. In most states the courts are actually organized around the county; judges are chosen at the local level and these courts have a distinctly local character.

At the base level of all court systems are the general trial courts where most trials begin. There are usually two kinds: municipal (city or county) courts, which handle misdemeanors (minor crimes such as vandalism) and civil cases involving a small amount of money; and county (circuit or district or superior) courts, which handle felonies and civil cases involving large amounts of money. The municipal courts usually have specialized branches such as probate or surrogate courts to handle wills and estates, small claims courts for financial claims under $1,000 or $500, juvenile or family courts, traffic courts, and—in rural areas or small towns— sometimes a justice of the peace.

The general trial courts handle thousands of cases that never come to public attention or make the newspaper unless they involve a scandal or a novel social issue. Judges have almost absolute control in making decisions, and only about 5 percent of the cases are ever appealed. A large portion of the business of the non-specialized municipal courts has to do with debt collection and tenant eviction.

Above this level most states have courts of appeal consisting of three to nine judges who decide appeals by a majority vote. There may be a single intermediate appellate court or regional divisions of the court. Above this is a state supreme court, also with a panel of judges who make the final decision on appeals. In half of the states any case can be appealed. The other states allow the higher courts to choose which cases they will hear. In deciding which cases to hear and by interpreting the state's laws and its constitution, courts can create state policy. Appeals can be taken to the federal courts only if the case involves a question of federal law.

Cases that reach the highest levels in state courts usually have some public significance. Lawyers and their clients wouldn't bother to appeal unless the stakes were worthwhile or the issue affected many people. Decisions by appeals courts are usually in writing and some of the judges may disagree and tell why. The appellate court judges generally serve longer terms than those in general trial courts and may be less responsive to changes in political influence in the state.

How the courts operate is seldom very clear to the layperson. Various courts often overlap both geographically and in the work they are responsible for doing. Or a single set of problems—such as a family or housing dispute—may require trips to several separate courts. Most state courts were created in a disorganized fashion as the need arose, and few have been abolished. One state may retain an orphans court long after it is needed and add a juvenile, traffic, or small claims court to handle more modern problems.

The chief justice of the state, who is usually elected by the other judges, has general authority to administer the courts and will try to insure uniform standards in the application of the law. Forty-two states have an administrative officer in addition to the chief justice. Lower-court systems may also select a presiding judge who controls the assignment of judges, the flow of cases, the rules of procedure, and the operating budget and physical facilities. In some lower-court systems, the presiding judgeship is rotated annually, often resulting in poor management.

CHOOSING STATE JUDGES

The single most important contributor to the quality of justice in the states is the judge. On a statistical basis the average state court judge in the early 1970s was Protestant and Anglo-Saxon, politically conservative, formerly active in politics, almost certainly a lawyer, male, and in his mid-fifties or sixties.

QUALIFIED JUDGES?

Most judges are elected through partisan elections (in twenty states) or nonpartisan elections (in eighteen states). In thirteen they are appointed by the governor and in five elected by the legislature—a carryover from the eighteenth century.* One candidate may have the endorsement of both parties, in which case the parties have agreed to divide the judgeships. The result is that the voter does not even have a choice.

Although judges are less subject to external pressures than executive officials and legislators, they often do not make completely objective, independent decisions. They are influenced by their political beliefs, personal values, and the necessity of being reelected.

A one-year study of all state and federal supreme court decisions that were not unanimous found that Democratic judges were more frequently in favor of defendants in criminal cases, state administrative agencies in business-regulation cases, tenants, in landlord-tenant disputes, labor unions in labor-management disputes, the debtors rather than the creditors, and the consumer in sale-of-goods cases.

Judges vary greatly in how long a sentence they give, too, depending on their personal beliefs about the seriousness of the crime, the chances of rehabilitation, or even on the race, social class, or occupation of the criminal.

Even though judicial elections are usually noncontroversial, judges are not unaware of popular sentiments. One West Virginia judge, responding to a questionnaire, admitted that as elections approached he postponed decisions in cases that might hurt his chances of reelection and hastily decided matters that might give him favorable publicity. Another state judge commented, "There is no harm in turning a politician into a judge—the curse of the

---

* This totals fifty-six because some states use different systems for selecting judges at different levels.

elective system is that it turns almost every elective judge into a politician."

Reformers urge that judges be appointed rather than elected, but there is little evidence that either method of selection produces better judges. Appointment does not necessarily eliminate political control; the governor can dole out judgeships in payment for support just as easily as the party can.

A plan to select judges on a merit principle was begun in Missouri in 1940. Under the so-called Missouri Plan the governor appoints judges to the highest courts from lists of nominees proposed by nonpartisan commissions of judges, laypeople, and lawyers. After an initial term the judges run for office without opposition. The voters simply vote yes or no to the question: "Shall the judge be retained in office?" They are almost always elected. Six states follow the Missouri Plan in selecting upper-level judges. The plan does not include metropolitan-level courts, which are most important to the political parties and most resistant to change.

The Missouri Plan has not removed from politics the selection of judges, however. The governor tends to select candidates of his or her own party from the list. And though the plan may take direct control of the nominating process away from the political party, it then gives undue attention to bar association recommendations for the positions. The danger here is that the bar may overemphasize professionalism and promote the wishes of the wealthier classes. Judges chosen by partisan methods are sometimes more responsive to existing social problems than judges chosen this way.

Although judges' terms vary from two years to life during "good behavior" (as in New Hampshire and Massachusetts), most trial judges serve about fifteen to twenty years—until they receive a higher office, die, or retire. Salaries range upward to over $50,000 for judges of the highest court in New York.

POLICE AND PROSECUTORS

Judges are not the only important officials in the judicial branch of state government. The police, for instance, have a great deal of power in deciding who is to be arrested in the first place. They act as judges in many situations, such as by choosing to ignore illegal behavior. The police also decide whether to concentrate on giving parking tickets, picking up drunks, or staking out a drugstore that has been plagued by robberies. What they crack down on may be determined by the mayor who appoints the chief of police or by the moral values of the community.

State police units, too, influence the judicial process. They began in the 1920s as state highway patrols, but today almost half of their work is general law enforcement. They are under the direction of a commissioner who is usually appointed by the governor.

Prosecutors are powerful because they usually determine which cases come to trial. The decision to prosecute usually depends on the strength of the evidence, but the case may be weakened if the police acted improperly in making the arrest. A prosecutor may be subject to strong political pressures and is sensitive to the moral values of the community. A prosecutor may choose to drop a case if prosecution would seem unjust. Violations of gambling laws, Sunday-closing laws, and housing codes are commonly ignored by both police and prosecutor if no one complains too loudly.

In some states the prosecutor must seek from a grand jury of six to twenty-three people an indictment for serious crimes. This prevents the prosecutor from initiating a case on his or her own for insubstantial reasons. Because prosecutors are often politically ambitious, they may try to gain publicity and build reputations as crusaders against sin or fighters against powerful interests. Robert La Follette, Thomas E. Dewey, and Earl Warren were outstanding prosecutors who went on to become governors and more.

OTHER FACTORS IN BRINGING A CASE TO TRIAL

Other factors may also affect which cases come to trial. Plea bargaining in criminal cases—pleading guilty to a lesser offense than what was originally charged—and out-of-court settlements in civil cases are as common as going to trial. Only about 10 percent of all criminal defendants plead not guilty and are tried. Most personal injury claims are resolved by negotiations between the parties. The property settlement in most divorce cases is worked out by the two lawyers involved who then ask the court to approve the agreement.

State court systems are so confusing and legal procedures so involved that most citizens cannot be very successful without a lawyer. Those unable to afford a lawyer, which includes most middle-income families, do not bring suits and many possible cases are never begun. The poor are seldom represented when they are defendants in civil cases, usually as tenants or debtors. Civil lawyers are more oriented in education and background to clients who can afford their services and who find them an essential part of conducting business.

Representation by a lawyer is so important in criminal cases that defendants who face a possible jail term of more than a few months are entitled to counsel at the government's expense if necessary. A recent study has shown, however, that in the lower criminal courts, the right to counsel is often not heeded. Increasingly, the poor are represented in civil or criminal cases by public defenders or by a local legal services office funded by the federal government.

The cost of legal proceedings—filing fees, witness fees, bail, paying to have a transcript made for an appeal—also discriminates against the person of average income. And once a citizen obtains a judgment in his or her favor, in small claims court for example, he or she may have trouble collecting the sum from the adversary.

The judicial branch of state government must also be concerned with the prison system of a state, although administration of prisons comes under the executive branch's control. Funds for prisons are usually last on a state's list of spending priorities, and federal judges in some states have found that prison conditions violated inmates' constitutional rights.

JUDICIAL REFORM

Despite the shortcomings of the judiciary, many people expect more from it in terms of assuring a just and humane society than they do from legislation or administrative rulings. Courts have been the last resort for victims of injustice and the only branch of government willing to make a decision on unpopular issues. If the courts are to justify the public's faith, some improvements are needed.

Perhaps the most important change would be to reduce the volume of cases the courts are expected to handle. In one year six million cases were filed in the California municipal courts: half were parking violations, and a large part of the rest were traffic cases. New types of cases such as worker's compensation, unemployment compensation, welfare, zoning, and urban development have been partly responsible for an increase in civil litigation. Because of the backlog in civil cases, delays of up to five years are possible, making reliable testimony difficult to obtain because witnesses have scattered. "Justice delayed" becomes "justice denied," especially for the criminal defendant who is unable to make bail.

One way to relieve the burden on the courts is to not prosecute "victimless" crimes. Six states have eliminated their public drunkenness statutes, so that the town drunk is not periodically hauled into court. Other actions sometimes considered victimless, when involving adults, and thus subject to decriminalization, are prostitution, gambling, homosexuality, marijuana use, and narcotics addiction.

Another way of reducing the caseload is to move minor offenses out of the courtrooms to less formal, quasi-judicial settings. Parking violation bureaus and small claims courts can perform this function, as well as making justice more accessible.

A second needed improvement is simplification of the court systems. No state seems to have an ideal organization, but one general recommendation has been to reduce the courts to three basic levels: general trial courts with statewide jurisdiction over every kind of case, supplemented by municipal or magistrates' courts below them to handle minor offenses and an appellate tribunal above them for questions of law.

Another suggested reform is to adopt standardized rules of procedure so that cases can be decided largely on their merits rather than on legal technicalities. It should also be made easier to remove dishonest or senile judges. One successful effort in this direction has been the California Commission on Judicial Qualifications, which was established in 1960 to hear and investigate complaints from private citizens. In its first four years it considered 344 complaints, which led to twenty-six resignations or retirements.

The jury system has been criticized as being costly, nonrepresentative, and adding to delay. Pools of jurors are drawn from the voter registration lists; the poor and minorities are often not registered. In some states juries are still chosen by the sheriff or another county officer and the jury's pay becomes a source of indirect patronage. A defendant may be faced not with a jury of peers but a jury of the sheriff's friends. In highly technical civil cases, juries have difficulty understanding the argument; indeed, the use of juries in civil cases has markedly declined. On the other hand, juries are often more sympathetic to the tenant in housing disputes than the judge.

Despite their predominance in the United States court system, it is obvious that the state courts are not and perhaps cannot be always equitable in the administration of justice. Some groups of the population will always be at a disadvantage. In general, the courts are conservative institutions that act as preservers of the status quo and as agents of the established social groups. In the process the disadvantages of the poor and minorities tend to be magnified.

CHAPTER FIVE

Political Parties and Interest Groups

The executive, the legislative, and the judicial branches make up the formal structure of state government. But the real power in the state often lies in political parties and interest groups. The power of these groups may not be obvious, since they often work behind the scenes. But the power of one group or party is more than the vote of any one legislator.

Party activity in the states usually follows one of four patterns: one-party dominance, two-party competition, modified one-party dominance, or nonpartisanship (having no political parties).

One-party dominance has been common in the states of the Deep South—Alabama, Georgia, Louisiana, Arkansas, Mississippi, South Carolina, and Florida—where Democrats prevail, and in upper New England—Maine, Vermont, and New Hampshire—where Republicans rule. In these states voters are most alike in the way they live and the way they think about politics. There is no great split between rural and urban areas, between strong ethnic groups, or between agriculture and industry. Instead, competition between factions (groups) of the dominant party is common. In Virginia the Byrd family, long active in politics, and an anti-Byrd group compete. In Louisiana a similar situation exists with the famous Long family. There may also be sectional divisions, as between the Piedmont and the Tidewater in the Carolinas or between northern and southern Vermont. Such groups are usually temporary and shifting and do not have the lasting quality or permanent ideas of political parties.

Strong two-party competition prevails most often in states such as New York and Illinois, ones that are characterized by a large number of cities, a high median income, a predominance of manufacturing, and a diversity of ethnic groups in the population. Where competition between the parties is strong, party organization is also strong. This is most common in states east of the Mississippi and north of the Ohio and Potomac rivers. But even in two-party states, some areas are always dominated by one party. Cities tend to be Democratic; rural and suburban areas tend to be Republican.

Less than one-quarter of the states have strong two-party competition. Seventeen have modified one-party dominance. In the border states of Kentucky, Maryland, and West Virginia, for instance, and the states of lower New England—Rhode Island, Connecticut, and Massachusetts—Democrats tend to prevail, but there is also a strong Republican party that occasionally captures the governorship or one house of the legislature. Strong two-party competition seems to be increasing, however, partly due to the effects of reapportionment.

A nonpartisan system—one without political parties—is most common in the Western states, which were organized in the late 1800s when feelings against political parties were strong. In writing their constitutions, Nebraska and Minnesota decided that state legislators would be elected without party labels. Party organizations exist in these states, but they are weak. Instead, interest groups have more power.

THE ROLE OF POLITICAL PARTIES

What do political parties accomplish in a state? Their main goal is to elect people to office—legislators, the governor, other executive officers, and judges. Once in office, their nominees can be counted on to vote with the party on many issues, to reward the party with appointments in the courts, executive branch, or on legislative staffs, and perhaps to favor party members in the awarding of highway construction contracts, liquor licenses, nursing home permits, and so on.

In theory, the most important function of the party, which derives from true two-party competition, is to take positions on issues so that they can be debated and resolved in a manner that gives the public a choice. The majority party tries to unite in support of a common program—usually the governor's legislative program if he or she is a member of that party. In the legislature, the dominant party promotes the bills it favors, using control of the steering committee, the leadership positions, and the majority of legislators. The opposition party then becomes the critic, choosing elements of the majority's program it wishes to oppose and forcing the majority party to defend them. Thus, the voter hears at least two views and can indicate his or her opinion in the next election.

In practice, it does not often happen this way. The parties are seldom divided on the important issues of the day, such as the budget—taxation and appropriations—education, health and welfare, regulation of business and labor, and the proper use of natural resources. Instead, both parties take a moderate position to avoid alienating any large group of voters. Even on issues peculiar to the state, such as whether the city of Denver should get its water from eastern or western slopes in Colorado, the parties don't like to take sides. They are far more likely to disagree on issues that affect their own internal operation and prestige: the organization of local government, the civil service, registration, and election laws.

There are other reasons for the parties' reluctance to take stands besides a desire to avoid offending voters. Some issues are so technical that the politicians doubt their ability to make the public understand. These decisions are then left to the administrators, lobbyists, and professionals who are involved in the matters.

Parties are also handicapped when there is divided partisan control in a state—when one party controls the executive and the other the legislature, when Republicans control one house and the Democrats the other, or when the long ballot has divided the executive offices between the parties. The most common situation of divided control is a Democratic governor with a Republican legislature, which can result in nonproductive conflict and a policy stalemate for which voters cannot blame either party.

On the national scene, state party organizations have a great deal to do with nominating the President and writing national party platforms. Governors, particularly, can control their delegations and deliver a vote for a Presidential candidate. They can even become a nominee themselves.

Because political parties devote more attention to putting people in office and to giving out patronage than to resolving issues and promoting good government, there have been a number of movements to take state government "out of politics." This effort began in the years after the Civil War, when the major force in American politics was a desire for office as a means of getting rich. One such movement resulted in the civil service system, which has steadily reduced the number of state jobs available for patronage. States also attempted to control the parties by setting organization and membership standards, regulating nominating procedures, and monitoring financial sources. In the large two-party states, state laws often spell out in detail how the parties may be organized, right down to the precinct level. As of 1974, all but three states regulate to some extent the amount and sources of contributions.

Because the states have the primary responsibility for elections in the United States, state parties have been able to turn this to their advantage. Voting requirements can be set up to prevent certain groups from voting in elections. The most common form of restriction was the one-year state residence requirement, which the Supreme Court struck down in 1972. Some five to eight million more people were allowed to vote as a result. Before the federal Voting Rights Act of 1965, Southern states used strict grading of literacy tests to keep blacks from voting.

Parties can influence the actual process of voting, too. James M. Curley, Democratic mayor of Boston in the 1940s, used to assign three voting machines to each Republican precinct, where long lines would form, and eight machines to Democratic precincts, so that no one would have to wait in a long line there.

On the whole, there is considerable disagreement as to whether partisanship helps or hurts state government. Thomas Brackett Reed, once speaker of the California house, said that "the best system is to have one party govern and the other party watch." But that type of partisanship has gone out of style. Party competition, when it exists, can allow the voter to hold someone or some group accountable for the conduct of state government, but the choices are seldom that clear.

Nonpartisanship has disadvantages, too. Voter interest in the elections decreases and interest groups become more powerful. This gives an advantage to upper and upper-middle income classes, who usually organize more effectively than the lower classes, which have traditionally depended on the parties. California, with weak parties and strong interest groups, has developed one of the best state government operations, with a high degree of nonpartisanship. But true nonpartisanship seems a very remote possibility in most states.

THE ROLE OF LOBBIES AND INTEREST GROUPS

Arthur H. Samish, the most notorious lobbyist in California history and probably in the country, once bragged that he was the governor of the legislature, and added, "To hell with the governor of the state." And at the peak of his activity throughout the 1930s and 1940s, few people disagreed that Samish really was "the real governor" of California. Samish represented a variety of industrial clients who were new to the state, and his goal was to keep them from being taxed; his organization resembled a very successful political party. People such as Samish, who promote the interests of groups to government officials, are called lobbyists (probably because they stand around a lot in lobbies trying to catch passing legislators).

Like the parties, interest groups influence state government in ways that are not always obvious to the general public. Despite the disappearance in recent years of blatant lobbyists such as Samish, interest groups are still so powerful that they have been called the "third house" of many state legislatures.

An interest group is any organized group that tries to influence the governmental process to benefit its members. Almost every citizen is represented by one interest group or another, whether it reflects the views of a profession or religion, a labor union or business, a veterans or minority rights group, or a branch of local government. More than two hundred organizations have delegates in the capital city of most states. Hundreds of others do not have a permanent delegate but send representatives as needed.

Whether an interest group is good or bad depends upon your point of view and upon the methods the group uses. An association of garage owners may attempt to exclude smaller garages from making major auto repairs; liquor store owners may sponsor a bill to prevent the sale of liquor in drugstores or wine in supermarkets; auto dealers may push for the right to sell car insurance and be opposed by insurance salespeople; a group of university professors may protest the closing of a graduate program by the state education board; an environmental group may file suit to block the construction of a highway through a wetlands area. All of these actions would be viewed favorably by some and unfavorably by others.

The largest and most effective lobbying groups in state government represent business and industry—manufacturers' associations, banks, railroads, truckers, insurance companies, realtors, trade associations such as the retail merchants associations, and particularly public utilities, liquor merchants, and horseracing, which are licensed and regulated by the state.

A business or industry group with its main resources or offices in one state will be particularly strong in that state's government. Mining companies kept legislatures in coal states from passing strong safety laws until disasters forced national legislation. In California the lumber interests were so strong that the national government had to step in to save the redwoods. The Anaconda Copper Company dominated government in Montana for years. Du Pont has been powerful in Delaware. Automobile manufacturers have a big impact in Michigan. In general, however, the development of different kinds of industries in states has reduced the power of once dominant companies.

Other types of interest groups that may be particularly effective in influencing state government are (1) farmers and farm organizations in agricultural states; (2) labor, which is strongest in the North and in urban areas; (3) professional groups, including the American Medical Association, bar associations, and the licensed professions; (4) veterans; (5) public employees; (6) religious, racial, and ethnic coalitions; (7) environmental protection groups; (8) consumers; (9) highway interests; and (10) good government and reform groups.

The citizen generally takes problems directly to the local or federal government and the politician sees state office as a way to national fame. Interest groups, however, concentrate on the state level, where they are most effective. Lobbyists have always flocked to state legislatures. In the 1974–75 session of the New York legislature, four hundred different interest groups spent more than $2.5 million on influencing legislation.

Lobbyists have earned a bad reputation, especially at the state level, for their attempts to influence officials with elaborate entertainment, threats of election defeat for nonconforming lawmakers, and outright bribery. But modern lobbyists are less visible and more subtle. They work in quieter ways that have proved more effective—informal communication with lawmakers, supplying information rather than applying obvious pressure, speaking at committee hearings and following up with personal contacts.

Although bribery is out of favor, lobbyists still use money to further their aims, mostly in the form of campaign contributions. An interest group may make a general contribution—labor regularly donates to the Democrats. Or a group may donate with a specific goal in mind, although that goal is seldom openly stated. The Pennsylvania Motor Truckers Association, for example, gave $76,000 to the campaign funds of various Pennsylvania legislators. The association was successful in gaining repeal of the state law limiting the weight of trucks on state roads to 45,000 pounds. This change improved their competitive position with respect to the railroads, who had strongly opposed the repeal.

In general, interest groups spend less money on the state than on the national level, but the state money goes farther. National interest groups may concentrate on affecting legislation in big states such as New York and California. A highway safety group was successful in getting the auto industry to supply seat belts in all the new cars they manufactured by getting New York State to require them in cars sold there.

Often a group does not even need to send a lobbyist to the legislature, because the group is already directly represented by some of the legislators. A banker-legislator or insurance executive–legislator helps write laws that favor his or her profession or business. Lawyers are particularly common in the legislature, although they don't always vote as a bloc.

Once favorable legislation has been passed, the lobbyist for an interest group must spend some time seeing that it is enforced by the executive branch. In addition to following through on legislation, interest groups may do their most important work in administrative offices, influencing appointments to the boards that regulate them.

Some interest groups, such as labor unions, may be weak in the legislature—because urban areas are still underrepresented there—but influential with the governor they helped elect. Governors, on the other hand, may be limited by the strength of interest groups in the legislature. Earl Warren and Edmund "Pat" Brown were both considered strong and socially progressive governors of California, but each admitted the superior power of the legislature's business constituency. "The lobbyists will go along with you on social legislation . . . ," Governor Brown said, "but if you want to get a truth-in-lending bill or improve insurance laws or get rid of price fixing, well, they are much stronger than the governor."

Interest groups have less influence with the judiciary, but they sometimes do finance suits and hire top legal talent to press their positions in court.

The influence of interest groups usually varies in relationship to the strength of political parties. When one is strong the other is weak. Among legislators interviewed in Massachusetts and North Carolina (older states with more entrenched political parties), only one-fifth said that lobbying frequently or occasionally changed

"I BELIEVE YOU'RE MAKING A BIG MISTAKE GETTING INVOLVED IN AN EMBEZZLEMENT. GOVERNORS JUST DON'T DEAL IN EMBEZZLEMENT. GOVERNORS TAKE BRIBES."

their mind. In the "new" states of Oregon and Utah, which have more open political systems, one-half the legislators said interest groups could change their minds. When parties are strong, interest groups must work through them. In Michigan, for example, labor and management identify with the Democrats and Republicans respectively.

There are both advantages and disadvantages to the input of interest groups. Among the advantages are that (1) they offer a kind of working representation to go with the geographic representation of the legislature; (2) they sometimes initiate good policies, pinpoint needs, and offer valuable criticism; (3) they pressure candidates to speak out on issues and thus also educate the public on the issues; and (4) they act as a unifying force between the different branches. The disadvantages have been more obvious. Even though lobbyists have refined and reformed their methods, in general they still speak for private rather than public interests. They are not responsible to the voters, some groups have more money and prestige than others, their internal operations are secret not public, and not every group (patients, as opposed to doctors, for instance) is represented.

The states have made some efforts to control lobbying. All forbid bribery, but enforcement is difficult and rare. Nearly all states force lobbyists to register and/or report the money they spend. Some legislatures have tried to adopt codes of ethics for both legislators and lobbyists with prohibitions against accepting excessive gifts or hospitality or receiving excessive compensation.

It is impossible and probably not desirable to do away with interest groups completely, but a careful eye must be kept on their activities. Fortunately, as public opinion has begun to play a bigger role in the votes legislators cast, interest groups have been forced to more carefully control their activities. Perhaps as they become even more visible, the public may better be able to define and protect its own interest.

CHAPTER SIX

A Closer Look at Some States in Action

Most Virginians, New Yorkers, Californians, Texans, and Vermonters can proudly recite some of the differences between their state and the others. The most obvious differences are in size and population. More significant are variations in wealth, usually stated as income per capita. The wealth of its citizens is the best single indicator of how much a state will spend on services. California, the largest state in terms of population, is also one of the wealthiest; as of 1974, its citizens' incomes totaled almost $2½ billion a week. California government, in turn, was spending $165 million a week, including more than $3 million a day on building and maintaining highways.

Spending differences between the states are actually very large. During the period 1973–74, Alaska spent the most per citizen—$2,501—in part because of its high cost of living. Arkansas spent the least, $609. One of the states with the highest per capita expenditures on public welfare—New York, at $213 in 1974—spent five times as much as one of the lowest—Arizona, at $40. Financial differences are also reflected in how much a state spends on its own government and the number of people it employs. In 1974 California employed 263,000 people and Wyoming 9,000. Their monthly payrolls were $1.135 billion and $17 million respectively. Generally, a state that can afford to do so will provide more for its citizens.

Some wealthy states—Illinois, Texas, Ohio, and Pennsylvania— keep their taxes low and thus rank relatively low in per capita expenditures. During the period 1973–74, Ohio ranked forty-ninth in taxes as a percentage of personal income, forty-eighth in expenditures for education, measured against ability to pay. New York, Arizona, South Dakota, Wyoming, and Wisconsin have relatively high tax burdens.

Wealth, size, and population aside, states also differ in the way in which they operate: the relative strength of their governors and legislatures, the influence of political parties and interest groups, the nature of their constitutions, and matters such as the amount of patronage a governor has to dispense. In the early 1970s in Illinois the governor and cabinet had 15,000 patronage jobs to give out, in California, 120, and in Iowa, 35.

The political tradition of a state is also important. Wisconsin has a reputation as a pioneer because of its leadership during the Progressive era. It was one of the first to adopt the direct primary, establish a legislative reference bureau, and provide worker's compensation. New York, Massachusetts, Michigan, Colorado, California, Louisiana, and Virginia also have reputations as innovators in their regions. Mississippi invented the sales tax, Oklahoma and Louisiana are relatively generous in their welfare expenditures, and Alabama spends a lot in old-age assistance. New York leads in educational innovation; Kansas has pioneered in mental health policies. California has emphasized rehabilitation in its prison system, with the result that the number of people who *return* to prison has been reduced to 35 percent (the national average is 50 percent).

It will be helpful to examine in some detail New York and Kentucky, two states that are very different from each other in many ways—in location, size, wealth, and the history and traditions of their people. Many facts true of these two states apply to the other forty-eight. The two states are indeed a study in contrasts.

NEW YORK STATE

Big, wealthy, with a large and varied population, New York is a state that prides itself on its political leadership. It has adopted many new programs and attempted to provide quality public services, but it has also often experienced problems first and worst. At its best New York is an example of how creative state government can make federalism work. At its worst it is an example of how crippled a state can become by its financial limitations.

New York has been blessed with leaders and has in turn passed them on to the nation. Theodore Roosevelt, Alfred E. Smith, Franklin D. Roosevelt, Thomas Dewey, Averell Harriman, and Nelson Rockefeller all got their executive experience as New York governors. The state's accomplishments during their administrations are impressive: consolidation of the executive branch into nineteen departments with the head of each appointed by the governor; one of the first executive budget systems; progressive labor laws; an emergency relief administration during the Great Depression; an early income tax; an extensive state university system; the nation's first fair-employment-practices law in 1945; the first consumer-protection law; a pure-water program in 1965; and the first state Council on the Arts.

New York is made up of a variety of geographic areas, and its people are of many races and nationalities. Sixty-three percent of the population lives in the New York City metropolitan area, but only 42 percent of these live within the city limits (the rest are in suburbs). The remainder of the state is invariably referred to as "upstate"—whether 100 or 350 miles from the city. Only 20 percent of the upstate population works in agriculture, although 37 percent of New York's acreage is farmland. The rest of the people work in manufacturing cities such as Buffalo, Syracuse, and Rochester; in the smaller cities of the Southern Tier; around the state capital, Albany; in towns along the Hudson River Valley; and in the rural areas of the Catskills, Finger Lakes, and North Country (the Adirondacks). The Adirondack Forest Preserve is the largest wilderness tract east of the Mississippi.

Political Profile

Politically, New York is two-party. As in most two-party states, the parties draw their votes from geographically distinct areas. Most of upstate New York—with the exception of Buffalo, the second largest city—is overwhelmingly Republican. New York City —with the exception of Staten Island—is overwhelmingly Democratic. The suburbs of the city usually vote Republican, but political offices are often closely contested.

Historically, control has alternated between the two parties. After the Civil War the Democratic party, based on a powerful political organization in New York City known as Tammany Hall, ruled the state with an iron but corrupt hand. Theodore Roosevelt and Charles Evans Hughes wrested control away from the Democrats during the Progressive era around the turn of the century and built a strong reform-minded Republican party. Under the leadership of Alfred E. Smith, FDR, and Herbert H. Lehman, the Democrats regained the governorship in the 1920s and 1930s as champions of the public interest against big business. The Republican party came under the domination of upstate utility and industrial interests and continued to control the legislature.

Thomas Dewey, who revived the tradition of progressive Republicanism, succeeded Lehman in 1943 and served three terms until Democrat Averell Harriman won a narrow victory in 1954 (partly because a big snowstorm upstate kept voters away from the polls). As the Tammany Democrats faded from the scene in New York City, the Republicans won again in 1958 with Nelson Rockefeller as governor, who remained in office for fifteen years. After Rockefeller resigned, Hugh Carey won for the Democrats in 1974. In Presidential voting, New York was strongly Republican from the 1890s to the 1930s, but the state has been more Democratic since Roosevelt's New Deal.

The brand of Republicanism practiced in New York has mostly been liberal. This means that New York Republicans have been more willing to use government to expand the opportunities and improve the welfare of all citizens, rich and poor, than have their fellow Republicans nationally. Since only 33.6 percent of New Yorkers consider themselves Republicans (as compared with 44.6 percent Democrats), the party depends on the uncommitted, independent voter (14.5 percent of the electorate)—a floating vote that Rockefeller was able to attract. Increasingly, too, Republicans have come to depend on the five counties around New York City, which constitute 15 percent of the state vote and remain more liberal in orientation than upstate counties.

Seventy-five percent of the Democratic vote is concentrated in metropolitan New York, a fact that causes the rest of the state to band together in opposition, no matter what their natural tendencies might be. This urban population is large enough to choose a leader for the whole state when it can unite behind a candidate. From 1918 to 1938, New York City pluralities elected ten of eleven governors. But New York Democrats in the recent past have not been known for unity.

Until a reform movement began in earnest in the 1950s, the Democratic party in New York was ruled by the political organization of Manhattan, Tammany Hall. It was often referred to as a "machine" run by "bosses." Boss control finally ended when Carmine DeSapio, the leader of Tammany in the 1950s, backed a series of losing candidates and simultaneously ended up in prison for corrupt practices in the early 1960s. Some bosses remain as county party leaders but they no longer have enough patronage to give out or the loyalty of ethnic followers to hold the machine together.

During the 1952 campaign of Adlai Stevenson for President, reformers decided to challenge the Democratic leadership in Manhattan. Eventually, a statewide organization—the New Democratic Coalition—was formed. This reform group won elections for liberal members of Congress throughout the 1960s and 1970s. It also forced the Democratic state committee to operate more democratically. The coalition now controls about one-quarter of the votes in the state committee. Competition between regular and reform Democratic groups has not contributed to a united front in elections. But the Democrats were able to fight out their differences in the 1974 primary and elect Hugh Carey governor.

Minor Parties

New York is unique in having two strong minor parties that attract a respectable portion of voters away from the major parties. The Liberal party was formed in 1944 as an anti-Tammany party, led by socialist-type union leaders who were mainly from the garment-making trade. The Conservative party was formed in 1962, in part to balance the Liberals on the right of the political spectrum. The Conservatives appeal mostly to a white, Catholic, middle-class homeowner constituency that was unrepresented in the liberal, big-government, high-taxes tradition of the two major parties. Their nominee for the Senate, James Buckley, was elected in 1970 but lost in his bid for reelection in 1976.

In general, a New York party must appeal to a fairly independent-minded electorate that is more concerned about issues and candidates than about party loyalty. The electorate has been described as thinking conservatively but acting liberally. In times of economic prosperity at least, it has been willing to support expanded state government programs. The one area of resistance has been to welfare.

New York Governors

New York ranks first among the states in the amount of power it gives to its governor. The governor's task as chief administrator has been made easy, for example, by dividing the executive branch into twenty departments with single heads or commissioners serving at the governor's pleasure. (The Department of Environmental Conservation was added in 1970.) Only the State Education Department is somewhat independent of the governor, because it is headed by a board of regents who are elected by the legislature. Since there is no limit on the number of successive terms a New York governor can serve (Rockefeller had four), each governor has a good chance of reelection. This possibility tends to make other executive officials more willing to cooperate with the governor in office.

In their relationships with the legislature, New York governors get the upper hand by making an executive budget, one that includes all the funds for education. They also have an item veto, including a provision that says the legislature may reduce the amount of any item in the budget but *not increase* any item without subjecting it to the veto. On general legislation a two-thirds vote is required to override the governor's veto. This happened in 1976—on a bill concerning funds for New York City schools—for the first time in 104 years. Most important legislation is passed in the last few days of the session; since the governor then has thirty days to sign or veto it, the legislature does not get a chance to override many vetoes.

Eight thousand state positions are exempt from the civil service, but the governor's patronage powers are more limited than this implies. Even though the governor appoints them, the commissioners of health, mental hygiene, and welfare are usually nominated by professional groups. Both the state university and Department of Mental Hygiene have a tradition of political independence and neither is usually influenced by patronage; mental hygiene appointments are controlled by the superintendents of various state hospitals. Democratic governors sometimes have trouble filling what patronage jobs they do have, because New York City Democrats are reluctant to move upstate just to work in state parks or for the New York Thruway Authority or even to accept an executive position that requires them to live in Albany.

New York's governors usually bring strong personalities to the job that further enhance its powers. Rockefeller used his immense personal wealth to finance opinion polls, an extensive, expert staff, and numerous campaigns.

The New York Legislature

The legislature in New York ranks second only to California's in professionalism. Its strong points include yearly unlimited sessions; control over its own time, staff, funds, and salaries; a wide range of staff services; uniform, published rules of committee procedure; and frequent, recorded and published roll-call votes in committees. The elected president of the senate and the assembly (the lower house) speaker have considerable power, including control of an annual legislative budget of $27 million. Among the New York legislature's faults are its long night sessions, crowded calendars, a circus atmosphere that develops at the end of each session when bills are rushed through, and a lack of rules preventing legislators from practicing before state regulatory agencies.

The legislature has usually been controlled by the Republicans. An exception was the Democratic sweep of both houses in 1964 and a Democratic assembly in 1974. It retains a somewhat conservative image, but despite its upstate domination has been willing to go along with many expensive and innovative programs, such as the provision of health services to low-income persons at a cost of $1.8 billion (in 1974) a year. Although the New York legislature has more independence than most, it, too, usually disposes of what the governor proposes rather than initiating its own programs.

Lobbying

Education is the biggest and most powerful lobby in the state. The board of regents has considerable control over the more than $2 billion in aid to local schools that the legislature gives out each year. The second most powerful lobby is industry, represented by the Associated Industries of New York and the Empire State Chamber of Commerce. Banks are influential, especially with upstate Republicans, and are well represented on the banking committees in the legislature. Organized labor is effective with New York City Democratic representatives. Organized medicine, the Catholic church, and the New York City lobby are also strong, although the church failed to sway a majority of its laypeople on the state's 1970 abortion reform law. It has been said that New York State government is so large that Albany draws lobbyists as flowers attract bees. Few interests go unrepresented there. Party discipline is strong in the legislature, however, and since the parties finance the election campaigns, they provide a balance to the influence of the interest groups.

Financial Troubles

New York's biggest problem now is paying the bill for its innovative programs, expanded social services, Rockefeller's extensive construction projects—sometimes referred to as his "edifice complex"—New York City's financial woes, and the social and economic burdens it has taken off the shoulders of many other states whose citizens migrated to New York. If the national government were to pay for welfare, New York, California, and Massachusetts alone would receive 51 percent of the money. In 1973 the state ranked first in amount of local taxes levied per person and third in state taxes ($447.30 per capita). Its budget doubled from 1970 to 1975.

New York's leaders have looked to Washington for financial help but have gotten little response. The state ranks forty-eighth in the percentage of its budget that is paid by the federal government. Although its per capita income is 20 percent higher than the national average, the cost of living is almost that much higher in the New York City area. The state's problems may be typical of other Northern and Eastern states which have lost population to the "sun belt" states of the South and West during the last ten years. With the population loss has gone part of the tax base, industries, and federal aid based on population. Temporarily, at least, innovation in New York seems to have come to a halt.

THE STATE OF KENTUCKY

In contrast to New York, Kentucky is moderate in size and population, and more rural than urban. Only 33 percent of its population lives in major city areas. It is one-party-dominated with a strong minority party, only modestly industrialized, relatively low in per capita income and state expenditures, and has more respect for tradition than for innovation.

GHOSTS OF CHRISTMAS PAST

Political Profile

Since the days of the Civil War, Kentucky has been considered a border state, which means, among other things, that the Democratic party does not dominate as completely as it has in the Deep South. The Civil War divided the populace and left its mark in the form of fierce party loyalties—Democratic in the agricultural, formerly slave-owning areas of central and western Kentucky, Republican in the southeastern, nonslave-owning mountain areas. Partisan feelings are less intense in the metropolitan areas along the Ohio River, areas such as Louisville and Jefferson counties (where one in five Kentuckians live), Lexington and Fayette counties in the heart of the Bluegrass country, and the suburban area south of Cincinnati.

Kentucky enjoyed a golden age after it was admitted to the union in 1792 with such leaders and natives as Henry Clay, Daniel Boone, Abraham Lincoln, and Jefferson Davis. A long decline followed its unhappy border position in the Civil War, but since World War II it has gradually begun to regain some of its luster. In 1974 the state was still 20 percent behind the national average in income per capita—ranking forty-first—and 20.8 percent of its housing had no plumbing facilities. Blue-collar, farm, and service equipment workers made up 60 percent of the population. Kentucky has been a fairly conservative state economically and socially (but not racially), whose isolation encouraged its people to look to politics for entertainment.

Democrats have predominated but the Republicans have always had 40 to 45 percent of the vote in Kentucky. Democrats have usually controlled the governorship—ten out of thirteen times from 1923 to 1971—and the legislature. But Republicans have done better in national elections, winning seven of ten senate races since World War II. Presidential voting has swung both ways;

the Democrats captured the state with Truman, Stevenson, and Johnson, the Republicans won with Eisenhower and Nixon. But with 66.6 percent of the people registered as Democrats, Democratic control over the state government has been firm.

As in New York, Kentucky Democrats have not been unified. The party is usually split in two: most primaries have been a contest between two candidates. The most persistent factions were those identified with the rivalry between A. B. "Happy" Chandler and Earle Clements, who each served as governor and as United States senator. Other politicians sometimes allied themselves with Chandler or Clements, but the political group in power is almost always opposed by another group trying to take the power for themselves. It is a game of the "ins" vs. the "outs." The governor leaving office tries to pick a successor and the group that is out of power unites behind a challenger.

Divisions among Kentucky Democrats have never reached the firmness of permanent political parties. Factions seldom take contrasting stands on issues or represent consistent social-economic interests. Voters often remain loyal to a particular candidate no matter what group the candidate is allied with.

Democratic strength lies in the rural western counties and in the Bluegrass area in central Kentucky. Democrats also attract conservative high-income city residents and blacks. The Republicans have drawn votes from the poor eastern mountain counties and the wealthy city areas; both constituencies tend to be conservative but vary greatly in their outlooks and backgrounds. The city counties have contributed most to recent Republican growth by providing funds, candidates, and organization. Democratic voters have become more independent and less devoted to traditional allegiances. As two-party competition increases and the Republicans become a respected opposition force, Democratic factionalism is expected to decline.

In the past in Kentucky the dominant party has used elections to hold its power. Gubernatorial elections have been held in off years, which helped the Democrats because the Republicans could not keep an organization going and raise funds without a Presidential election. And the Democrats have reportedly assessed state employees 2 percent of their salaries to be donated to the party. As spoils have gradually become less important and with the introduction of voting machines and a computerized registration system in 1973, Kentucky politics have become "cleaner." The legislature passed an election finance registry law but it has not been vigorously enforced yet.

Kentucky's closed primary, in which a voter can vote only for candidates of the party he or she declares an affiliation with, has also helped the Democrats. Since the Democratic primary results usually determine the governorship, Republicans have registered as Democrats in order to be able to influence the choice of candidates. They cannot then vote in the Republican primary. As a result, the Republican nominee has often been selected by the mountain areas.

Kentucky Governors

The governorship in Kentucky has been strong but for different reasons than in New York. Rather than exercising extensive formal powers, the Kentucky governor has benefitted from use of patronage and from the weakness of the legislature. Some formal powers have been used to advantage. Governor Wendell Ford, elected in 1971, consolidated the state's executive departments. He already had the authority to appoint and remove agency heads without the approval of the senate. One fact that works against a strong governorship has been that the governor and other executive officers may not succeed themselves (a provision written into the constitution when a state treasurer fled with a quarter of a million dollars after twenty years in office). This has caused a great deal of hopping around between jobs.

About four thousand (of twenty thousand) state jobs are not covered by the merit system and can be filled by the governor. The largest group are some three thousand for unskilled laborers and light-equipment operators in the highway department. There are also jobs available in the state parks—especially summer jobs— and as teachers, coaches, bus drivers, janitors, etc., which are channeled through the local school superintendent. This number of political jobs is unusual for education.

In addition to jobs, the governor can hand out highway construction projects, parks, community colleges, and hospitals to the counties and state business to legal firms or insurance companies. The state treasurer determines which bank receives deposits of state funds. Patronage has declined in Kentucky as a result of the merit system, low pay for professionals, and federal controls on federally funded projects, but it remains an all-important tool for the governor.

Kentucky governors have also been strong party leaders. Because the 120 counties are the important units of government, the governor chooses a contact person in each county, often a campaign manager there, to handle problems and requests. The contact person delivers the county's vote on election day and the governor delivers the patronage.

An example of how former governor Chandler used patronage to gain a vote for his budget is related by a Republican from eastern Kentucky: "One of the five National Guard armories in the state is in my county—a Republican county—even though several large Democratic counties were trying hard for it. Why was I able to get it? Chandler's budget passed by one vote and I voted for it."

In his role as legislative leader the governor depends primarily on the support of party members and the weakness of the opposition. He or she has the power to call special sessions and a veto that is almost impossible to override.

The Kentucky Legislature

Although the Kentucky general assembly is gradually becoming stronger, it has suffered from a bad case of "constitutional malnutrition." It is limited to one regular sixty-day session every two years. This schedule allows little time for any serious consideration of legislation. Most of the session is given to the governor's program and very little to bills proposed by its own members. Committees report on major legislation within a day or two of receiving it. About half of the legislators do not even seek reelection. Salaries are an estimated $12,350 for two years' service, a little below the national average. Annual legislative sessions were rejected by the voters in 1973.

The legislature is weak because it is not a unified, independent critic of the executive branch. Republicans have never won a majority in the senate and have controlled the house only twice, in 1895 and 1919, thus providing no consistent opposition. Many legislators are much more concerned with getting state projects than with taking a stand on an issue, as illustrated by the delegate from the county with a National Guard armory. If the Republicans continue to gain in the state, they may strengthen the legislature.

Certain interest groups have been consistently strong in Kentucky. At the turn of the century it was the railroads—especially the Louisville and Nashville Railroad—the tobacco industry, whiskey distillers, the Jockey Club representing racing interests, schoolbook and insurance companies, and coal mining companies. During the New Deal the economy became more diversified and the railroads weaker. The United Mine Workers came out in opposition to the mining companies, and teachers assumed more importance through the Kentucky Education Association.

Racing, liquor, and tobacco are still the strongest economic interests of the state, as well as coal and a rural electric cooperative movement. Tobacco is grown in every county in Kentucky, producing $350 million in sales annually, and it is not coincidental that Kentucky has a low tax on cigarettes. Coal is mined in 55 of the 120 counties and there was no strip-mining control legislation or severance tax on the production of coal until 1966. The *Louisville Courier Journal* newspaper is a liberal force in the state.

Kentucky has a balanced and progressive tax system, including income, sales, and corporation taxes, but practically the lowest property taxes in the country. The fact that it ranks forty-fifth in tax collections (thirty-eighth as a percentage of personal income) is reflected in its expenditures. Kentucky is forty-sixth in per capita spending on local schools, forty-third on health and hospitals, forty-second on police protection, twenty-third on welfare, and seventeenth on highways (in contrast to New York, which ranks last on highway spending). Its state park system, however, is one of the best in the nation. The state has not experienced the severe financial difficulties of the larger states, in part because rising coal prices have helped preserve a budget surplus.

One of the state's most serious lags has been in providing education. In the 1970 census Kentucky ranked last in the median number of school years completed by adults—9.9 as compared to the national average of 12.1. But in the 1960s, state and federal funds spent for education increased from $62 million to $226 million. The University of Kentucky was expanded and thirteen community colleges have been built in recent years.

Kentucky State government has not been an innovator and does not provide a great many services to its citizens. But it is in the process of becoming a more positive force. With a growth of cities and a loss of population in the rural areas, levels of income and education have increased. These factors, plus exposure to television, are changing voting patterns that were once predictable. Kentucky is typical of many states whose goals have been modest but whose economic and political development is on the upswing.

COOPERATION AMONG STATES

Despite their differences the states cooperate in a number of formal and informal ways. All look to their neighbors for new ideas and information on similar problems. A program may be passed on from one state to another until it becomes recognized as a common responsibility. The actions of one state are bound to affect another. In the early 1970s, for example, Connecticut decided to ban aerial spraying with certain pesticides such as DDT. Rhode Island and New York continued to use them, however, and the sprays carried across the borders, killing desirable insects and undoing much of the benefit of the ban. After discussions both states eventually agreed not to spray within 1,000 feet of Connecticut's borders.

According to the Constitution the states are forbidden to erect trade barriers—import or export duties on goods—between themselves or to make interstate agreements without the consent of Congress, but exceptions have been necessary. Congress compelled certain states to participate in the Tennessee Valley Authority (the TVA), which uses the power of the Tennessee River to provide electricity throughout the Tennessee Valley region.

The states themselves have also asked permission to form interstate compacts to pool their resources or share administrative responsibilities. Examples of this kind of cooperation are the Port Authority of New York, the Upper Colorado Basin Compact, and the Southern Regional Education Board.

Governors also often meet formally or informally to discuss common problems. The national Governors Conference, formed in 1908, meets yearly to discuss politics, lobby Congress on behalf of the states, and exchange information. Other interstate groups attempt to recommend uniform laws affecting transactions between citizens of different states. By acting together, the states are often able to assert more power and carve out a more positive role for themselves in the federal system.

CHAPTER SEVEN

The Sleeping Giant?

Will state government ever fade away completely? Some say yes. "The American State is finished," Luther Glick, a specialist in public administration, wrote in 1933. David Brinkley predicted in 1970 that the states would disappear in twenty-five years. "The United States has been for a long time now becoming the United State," writes Martin Landau, a political scientist. And Senator Everett Dirksen of Illinois once predicted that "the only people interested in state boundaries will be Rand McNally."

Others say no. Former Oregon governor Mark O. Hatfield asserts that "the states are not on the governmental junk-heap." Former Pennsylvania governor William Scranton called state government "the sleeping giant of the past few decades," implying that it only needs to wake up to become a strong and positive force.

If the states are dying, the reasons are laziness and neglect. In part these reflect the fact that the American public seems to have lost faith in state governments. When asked which news they follow most—national, local, international, or state—respondents answered in that order. State government makes news only when gossip or a scandal is related: the governor's wife asks for divorce or the secretary of state is indicted for bribe-taking. Accomplishments are either few and far between or do not achieve the media attention they deserve.

There has been a great change, since the writing of the Constitution, in the states' position in the federal system. In the twentieth century power has flowed to the national government, either because it was "grabbed" by Washington or because it drifted there without opposition by the states. The national government has assumed a dominant role in areas formerly left to the states— in highways under President Eisenhower, in housing and social welfare under President Kennedy, and in education and ecology under President Johnson. In 1957 President Eisenhower explained why this was occurring: "In each instance state inaction, or inadequate action . . . has forced emergency federal action."

But at the same time that the national government was expanding its areas of activity and increasing its spending, states were spending more, too. More state revenues began to flow to local communities. The national government's support has settled at about 31 percent of total spending for domestic activities. The states have increased their share of spending from 30 percent in 1946 to 48 percent now.

GRANTS-IN-AID

A major modern development affecting national-state relations has been grants-in-aid—money given by the federal government to the states. Since the 1930s grants-in-aid have provided money to be used for a specific purpose. The states must often "match" the grants with some money of their own, and usually the states administer the program. The national government sets some rules, such as selecting employees by a merit system, and sets requirements for such things as the quality of materials to be used.

The Federal Highway Aid Act of 1956, for example, provided that if a state government spent 10 percent for the cost of a highway, the national government would pay 90 percent. Similar city renewal programs provide 75 percent of the cost of a local program. Naturally, such programs encourage the states to build highways and to start city renewal projects.

Grants-in-aid are helpful because they enable states to spend money in areas they could not afford on their own. They give the money from national income taxes to poorer states and to sometimes neglected services, such as education, hospital construction, public works, and city renewal. Orville Freeman, while governor of Minnesota (1956–1960), commented that "federal grants-in-aid have certainly increased, not decreased, the scope of state activities." And through requirements for the merit selection of staff, they have upgraded the quality of state government operations.

Federal programs vary greatly in their impact, however, and their chief disadvantage is that they attempt to impose uniformity. The United States Bureau of Public Roads requires, for example, that on federally funded highways the center and side lines must be painted white. But white lines are not as safe as yellow lines in a state like Wyoming. "Let them come out here and find one of their white lines during one of our blizzards," commented a state official who had unsuccessfully requested permission to change the color.

Grants for a specific purpose also deny states the flexibility they need to plan well. A public health nurse in Florida, who is financed by a special federal heart fund, is not supposed to aid cancer and tuberculosis patients in the households she visits. If the state wants to provide services to victims of these illnesses, a different nurse must make a completely separate visit.

One federal program that does allow a great deal of flexibility is the Clean Air Act of 1971. Under its provisions, the Environmental Protection Agency establishes national air quality standards and sets the timetables for compliance by the states. But the states come up with their own plans to meet the standards. By contrast, the Clean Water Act of 1972–73 spelled out exactly how the states were to carry out water pollution control. Connecticut environmental protection commissioner Donald Lufkin said that his staff spent 50 percent of its time answering questions from the federal agency rather than combatting pollution.

Other disadvantages are that federal programs overlap and are uncoordinated, so that it is difficult for a state to decide which of four hundred different grants it should apply for. Burdensome reporting procedures often require a mountain of paperwork, and there are delays in getting decisions from regional and national offices. Many states have difficulty making out their budgets because they don't know how much federal money they will be receiving. Federal appropriations are made on an annual basis and state budgets are usually on a two-year basis.

A more subtle drawback to the grants is that they can lure a state into spending money for services that do not really match its own needs. North Carolina governor Terry Sanford commented in his book *Storm over the States* that "priorities are reordered to suit the money available, forcing states to meet grants instead of meeting problems." For example, federal funds available under the Highway Beautification Act of 1965 were used to plant non-indigenous trees and shrubs—purple-flowering crabs, Australian pine, Japanese black pine, and forsythia—on a bed of wood chips along a stretch of highway on Cape Cod, Massachusetts. The highway already overlooked marsh, heather, dune, and ocean. Whether or not this further beautification was a state priority, the money was available and so it was spent.

Revenue-sharing—the new federalism of the 1970s—was in part

an attempt to get around the disadvantages of grants-in-aid by returning federally collected income directly to the states to use as they wished, with no particular programs required. But its impact has been minimized as the cost of state services continues to spiral. Revenue-sharing funds are swallowed up quickly.

LOCAL GOVERNMENT

As the states' relationships to the national government have changed, so have their relationships to localities. According to the Constitution, local governments are subordinate to the states, but a strong tradition of home rule has always prevailed, a tradition that is akin to the states' rights position with the national government. Yet only the states may exercise certain powers that affect local government. The states must approve new combinations of city and county government, give and take away taxing authority, and set local property tax rates. The states are particularly important to medium-sized and small communities, which do not have enough political clout to take their problems directly to Washington.

Financially, the states contribute about 35 percent of funds used locally, which accounts for more than a third of all state expenditures. States vary in the percentage they return to local governments: Minnesota and New York allocate 50 percent of their state budgets; Hawaii returns only 3 percent.

The weakest link in state-local relationships has been with the growing city areas. In 1970 two-thirds of the U.S. population lived in metropolitan communities with core cities of at least fifty thousand people. The states have failed to keep up with city problems. In 1962 less than 2 percent of state aid to localities went for housing and planning and nothing was spent on mass transit.

This neglect forced the cities to bypass the states and appeal directly to the national government. A fighting relationship resembling guerrilla war developed between some states and their largest cities. Novelist Norman Mailer even suggested in his 1969 campaign for mayor that New York City secede from New York State. City governments often want only power and money from the states, however, with no strings attached.

The states will be forced to take more responsibility in city affairs, as the national government continues to spend more of its money outside the United States. There is much that the states could do. An Advisory Commission in Intergovernmental Relations was created by Congress in 1959 to study the city environment. It advised that "the states must buy their way back into the urban areas" by providing adequate state revenues and streamlining local tax structures, including the equalization of local property taxes. (By 1970, in twenty-two states local governments collected a sales tax and in eleven states an income tax.) They must grant local governments adequate legal powers, the right to add area to the town or city, and the right to plan for large areas.

STATE TAXATION

The states have begun to feel a financial pinch as more and more is demanded of them. In the last two decades state taxes have increased sharply. In 1969 more than three-quarters of the states raised taxes; the rate of increase was almost as high in 1971, tapered off in 1973, and has risen again. But the increases have not really helped, because the states rely on taxes that do not increase with inflation as much as the federal income tax does. The states also use taxes such as the sales tax, which fall heavily on those least able to pay.

States have begun to rely more on the personal income tax. It is regarded as the best kind of tax because it matches the ability to pay; it also responds better than the sales tax in an expanding economy. But the sales tax, including taxes on gasoline, cigarettes, and so forth, still accounts for more than half of state revenues.

There is also an element of competition between the states; they try to keep corporate taxes lower than their neighbors, in order to attract industry. Florida repealed its inheritance and estate tax law in 1924 so that the wealthy would be encouraged to retire there, and Nevada followed suit in 1925. States rich in natural resources manage to shift some of their tax burden out of state by taxing iron mines (in Minnesota) or oil (in Louisiana). The increased cost of the resource is passed on to nationwide consumers.

Despite their willingness to tax more in order to provide more services, the states have not been able to keep up with demand. Their economic growth rates have slowed, and tax receipts have declined at the same time that demands for services have increased. In New York the state budget doubled in the five years between 1970 to 1975 and then slowed down. California's budget is now growing at the rate of 6 percent rather than the 12 percent average of the past eight years.

Governors are still asking for higher taxes to cover budget deficits and are being turned down by the legislators and defeated by the voters. The public has become much less willing to approve bond issues: in 1958–60 they approved 80 percent of public school bond issues and in 1970 only 44 percent. Gone are the "golden growth days of the 1960s," according to California Governor Edmund G. Brown, Jr., when everyone could afford at least one new highway. Some of the most severe cutbacks have been in state employee payrolls, Medicaid payments—especially for dental work and prescription drugs—education, and welfare.

The financial problems of the states increase demands for greater federal responsibility. The national government now pays 60 percent of welfare costs; some say it should pay all so that the

"NEXT WINDOW, PLEASE."

costs do not fall more heavily on states that attract poor residents from other states. The same reasoning can be used to argue that the states should assume all costs for education because localities raise unequal amounts from their property taxes.

Whether the states or the national government should take the lead in spending or in legislating often depends on the particular issue at hand. Florida's governor LeRoy Collins commented on the use of the states' rights argument as a smokescreen: "Those economic interests which have opposed—in the name of states' rights—every single effort at the federal level to provide American citizens assurance of decent minimum wages have not encouraged the state governments to provide such. It is not really 'federal encroachment' they oppose: it is minimum wages."

The states have undoubtedly been backward in civil rights and voting rights; liberals have looked to Washington to right injustices in these areas. On the other hand, individual states have often been the first to act in areas such as pollution control, women's rights, prison reform, mental health, and highway safety. All fifty states established consumer protection offices before Congress. And as the national government became more conservative during the 1970s, liberals began to back off from federal action as it took the form of antibusing statutes and antiabortion amendments.

CONSTITUTIONAL REVISIONS

Aside from financial limitations and the involvement of the national government, the states have been hamstrung by internal weaknesses that have been discussed in the preceding chapters. An obvious place to start internal reform is with the state constitutions.

The majority of today's state constitutions, which were drafted in the nineteenth century, have stifled the growth of the states because of their excessive detail, restrictive nature, and difficult amendment procedures. Rather than providing broad outlines for policy within which state officials can react to changing times, as the national Constitution does, the constitutions often spell out exactly what the state can and cannot do in all possible situations. The Oklahoma constitution, for example, requires the teaching of home economics in all public schools, rather than leaving curriculum to the state education department or even to the legislature. The California constitution limits the powers of the legislature concerning the length of wrestling matches. The Louisiana constitution at 236,000 words is half as long as *Gone with the Wind* but not half as interesting.

Many constitutions set maximum tax rates and establish so many earmarked funds that less than half of all state revenues may be available to the legislature to spend. Further, constitutional debt limitations prevent the states from using deficit financing as extensively as the national government does.

Powerful interest groups, in particular, try to write protection into the constitution in such forms as a special exemption from taxation for veterans, labor unions, farmers, church groups, or the gasoline industry. The Connecticut constitution provides a home office deduction for insurance companies—there are a lot of insurance headquarters in Connecticut—and requires a two-thirds vote to alter business taxes.

The fact that state constitutions are detailed encourages state judges to say that anything not expressly permitted in the constitution is unconstitutional. This, in turn, encourages constant amendment. The most common procedure is by a two-thirds vote of the legislature and a majority of the popular vote in the next election. On the other hand, it is so difficult to amend the constitution in Tennessee that not one amendment was added between 1870 and 1953.

It is hard to excite voters about constitutional change. When a new constitution was voted down in Maryland in 1968, it was the fourth to be rejected in five years. Piecemeal approaches, whereby voters are asked to approve small reform provisions, have been more effective.

REFORMING STATE GOVERNMENT

Reforming the three branches of state government also has been quite difficult to achieve, as discussed in preceding chapters. The legislature is reluctant to change, has many issues to consider other than its own reform, and fears a redistribution of power even though it has little in most states. Governors, too, may not be enthusiastic about a more independent legislature that threatens their own power. Partisanship has been blamed for holding back the legislatures from reform. Former speaker of the California assembly Jesse Unruh has advocated one-house legislatures to make them less expensive and more effective. "I suspect that a one-house legislature of around a hundred members could save as much as 30 to 40 percent of the present two-house costs in California and that most other states could show comparable savings," he says.

The executive branch has been ahead of the legislative in gaining such measures as the executive budget, the short ballot, and the four-year term with the right to a second term. Improved salaries have been effective in upgrading the quality of state employees. The governor of New York now has an annual salary of $85,000, followed by Texas at $65,000 and Pennsylvania at $60,000. Arkansas pays the least, at $10,000.

Change is also needed in the judicial branch. No method of selecting judges has proved clearly superior to another, and it has been extremely difficult to remove the courts from political influence. (It took a twelve-year campaign in Illinois to reform the courts because of opposition from the parties.) Among the obstacles to judicial reform are lawyers who have a vested interest in keeping the courts complex, court officials who don't want to lose their jobs, and city politicians who would lose patronage to pass out. Standing in opposition to this is only a vague feeling among the general public that the courts should be better than they are.

As a reaction to political parties that offer no clear-cut choice on state issues and are concerned largely with the spoils of office, two states have tried nonpartisanship. Minnesota and Nebraska have made elections for the legislature, half of local offices, and a quarter of judicial elections nonpartisan. But nonpartisanship is not widely viewed as a reasonable alternative to the prevailing two-party system. Likewise there seems to be little chance of eliminating interest groups, but better chances of regulating and containing their efforts. The best way seems to be the competition of other interests.

Ironically, one decision by the Supreme Court—to force the states to reapportion their legislatures—may do more to help the states regain their vitality than any single action they could have taken on their own. By bringing in a new and younger membership from formerly underrepresented people, reapportionment may encourage a stronger, more independent legislative branch.

If the states reform their internal governmental structures and change their financial systems, they may be able to reestablish a stronger position in the federal arrangement. Overall, the trend seems to be in the direction of less dependence on the national government and more reliance on the states. Federal aid as a percentage of state and local revenues fell back in 1974 despite revenue-sharing. Big government and big spending as represented by the national government may be going out of style.

If the state initiatives continue, there will be a renewal of these smaller units of government, for they can be held more closely responsible to the voters for the use of the taxpayers' money. Indeed, the residents of Upper Michigan would like to create a new fifty-first state—the state of Superior—an indication of the desire for less-centralized government. With new vitality the states may become once more, as Madison described them, the primary power governing the "lives, liberties, and properties of the people."

BIBLIOGRAPHY

Adrian, Charles R. *Governing Our Fifty States and Their Communities.* 2d ed. New York: McGraw-Hill, 1967.

American Assembly. *State Legislatures in American Politics.* Edited by Alexander Heard. Englewood Cliffs, N.J.: Prentice-Hall, 1966.

*Buechner, John C. *State Government in the Twentieth Century.* Boston: Houghton Mifflin, 1967.

*Committee for Economic Development. *Modernizing State Government.* New York, 1967.

Council of State Governments. *The Book of States, 1974–1975.* Lexington, Ky.

*Fesler, James W., ed. *The Fifty States and Their Local Governments.* New York: Knopf, 1967.

Halacy, D. S., Jr. *Government by the States: A History.* Indianapolis: Bobbs-Merrill, 1973.

Jacob, Herbert, and Vines, Kenneth N., eds. *Politics in the American States.* 2d ed. Boston: Little, Brown, 1971.

Lockard, Duane, ed. *Governing the States and Localities: Selected Readings.* New York: Macmillan, 1969.

*Indicates books geared to younger readers.

*Peirce, Neal R. *The Border States*. New York: W. W. Norton, 1975.
*————. *The Megastates of America*. New York: W. W. Norton, 1972.
*Sanford, Terry. *Storm over the States*. New York: McGraw-Hill, 1967.
*Sharkansky, Ira. *The Maligned States*. New York: McGraw-Hill, 1972.

ABOUT THE AUTHOR

Judith Bentley is a free-lance writer, who among other activities contributed to Ralph Nader's *Congress Project,* and also has held editorial positions with Newsweek Books and the *Saturday Review.* She is a graduate of Oberlin College and earned her master's degree in the History of American Civilization at New York University. Mrs. Bentley, who lives with her husband and daughter in Brooklyn, teaches at New York City Community College.